*Handbook for Research
in American History*

Handbook for Research in American History

A Guide to Bibliographies and Other Reference Works

Second Edition, Revised

Francis Paul Prucha

University of Nebraska Press
Lincoln and London

Library of Congress Cataloging-in-Publication Data
Prucha, Francis Paul.
Handbook for research in American history:
a guide to bibliographies and other reference
works / Francis Paul Prucha.—2nd ed., rev.
p.   cm.
Includes index.
ISBN 0-8032-3701-4 (cl).—
ISBN 0-8032-8731-3 (pa)
1. United States—History—Bibliography.
2. Bibliography—Bibliography—
United States.   I. Title.
Z1236.P78   1994
[E178]
016.973—dc20
93-4240   CIP

To the librarians of the
Marquette University Library and
the Milwaukee Public Library,
who have helped me in
countless ways

Contents

Preface to First Edition, 1987

In dealing with graduate students in American history over a period of more than a quarter century, I have sought to develop in them a professional sense. Intelligent use of library resources has been a major objective in that undertaking, and I have directed the students to many of the basic reference works that they will need in order to find materials for advanced reading and research. The guides that my students and I have used are now outdated, and I have felt the need for a reasonably complete and up-to-date work to replace them, at least in part. That is the reason for this *Handbook*.

I have been helped in the enterprise by many skilled reference librarians in the Marquette University Library, Milwaukee Public Library, Library of Congress, National Archives, Huntington Library, Newberry Library, and University of California, Los Angeles, Library. Special assistance came from Robert M. Kvasnicka of the National Archives and from Ralph E. Ehrenberg and Ronald E. Grim of the Geography and Map Division of the Library of Congress. History colleagues, too, have offered advice and encouragement. To all of them I offer my sincere thanks.

A summer fellowship at the Huntington Library in 1986 enabled me to put most of the finishing touches on the book, especially in checking and rechecking physically the many items listed.

Preface to Second Edition, Revised

The years since the publication of the first edition of this *Handbook* have been busy ones for American history bibliographers. Not only have there been new editions of standard reference works, but new electronic technologies have greatly augmented the possibilities for searching out materials. Libraries and archives, the traditional storehouses of information for research, are undergoing rapid changes, so that the environment in which the researcher works is different and will continue to change. To bring graduate students and other scholars in American history abreast of these challenging developments, a new and revised edition of the *Handbook* seemed worthwhile.

The revision retains the general structure and purpose of Part One of the original *Handbook,* while adding new publications, updating information on older ones, and expanding the discussion of some that have become more important. New attention is paid throughout to guides available now in electronic form.

Part Two of the first edition—bibliographies of bibliographies on selected topics—is omitted altogether in the revision. The two genres of Part One and Part Two are not necessary for each other and do not fit well together in a single volume. Bringing the topical bibliographies up to date would have increased the length of the revised *Handbook* to the extent of endangering its purpose, that is, the introduction to selected reference materials of different types, which formed the substance of the former Part One. Researchers who understand the use of the reference works discussed here can easily enough prepare bibliographies, or even bibliographies of bibliographies, for topics of their choice.

I again thank the librarians, archivists, and history colleagues who assisted me with the first edition and now extend the thanks to those who have aided in the preparation of the second edition. They have added much to my knowledge and have steered me clear of pitfalls.

Francis Paul Prucha, S.J.
Marquette University

Introduction

Historians build on the works of those who have gone before them. Hundreds of men and women have searched out sources, analyzed and digested them, and in many cases used them as the basis for the reconstruction of past events—written history. Others have made it their task to assemble large numbers of items, classified by subject, author, or place, and to list them in catalogs, checklists, or bibliographies for the convenience of others.

Researchers in American history must learn to use the variety and multitude of such catalogs, bibliographies, guides, and other reference books. Beginning historians must be introduced to the materials that await them in the reference sections of the library. Some of the works discovered will become constant companions; others may be needed only occasionally or not at all.

The *Handbook* deals principally with categories of material, from library catalogs, through manuscript, newspaper, and other guides, to legal sources and oral history. It includes, as well, chapters to direct researchers through the maze of documents in the printed records of the federal government and the voluminous manuscripts in the National Archives. In most chapters, general guides are listed first; these may be all that the researcher will need. Then reference works for specific kinds of material or particular subjects are listed for those who might find use for them. The *Handbook* is, in a sense, a bibliography of bibliographies and other reference works, which will in turn direct the researcher to useful books, articles, and other sources. Only in a few instances—notably the chapter dealing with published documents of the federal government—does it point to the sources themselves.

Since the early 1960s the number of bibliographical guides for American history has multiplied greatly. This growth is due in part to the creation of electronic databases, which store vast amounts of bibliographical data and from which bibliographies on many specific subjects can be called up and published. (See chapter 1 for more detailed information on electronic access.) A number of publishers have specialized in issuing bibliographies and other reference guides. ABC-Clio, with large databases of bibliographical abstracts, has drawn on them for specialized as well as general bibliographies, and Gale Research has produced computer-generated bibliographies and indexes as well as guides to information sources on a variety of topics. G. K. Hall and Company in the 1960s and 1970s flooded libraries with multivolume folio sets that photographically reproduced the card catalogs of entire libraries or of special collections. Scarecrow Press, Meckler, Garland Publishing, and Greenwood Press, among others, have turned out what seems to be an endless array of bibliographies, often in ongoing series devoted to particular areas of study. Not all of these, of course, are of the highest quality; some seem hastily thrown together, with carelessness in citation or with illogical or confusing classifications. But taken as a whole, they offer remarkable bibliographical coverage for materials on American history. Professional organizations, too, like the American Library Association, the American Historical Association, the Organization of American Historians, and many state and local libraries and historical societies have furthered the cause with new publications and with task forces investigating new topics or innovative methods.

The newer works do not always replace older ones; many merely add new entries to previous lists and do not provide an updated cumulation. But this *Handbook,* by and large, does not include all the older and still useful publications, to which one can gain access through standard guides to reference books or such bibliographies as the *Harvard Guide to American History* [114] or Beers's *Bibliographies in American History* [124] and [125].

The listing of titles here is not intended to be exhaustive. The field of American history is too broad and the books too numerous for any such pretentions. New editions of older works and brand-new reference books, too, are easy to miss because of oversight, and some titles, no doubt, have been omitted because of poor judgment. Enough is included, however, to give a researcher a substantial start and to point the way to other guides.

Nor can the reference works cited in the *Handbook* be considered definitive. With the explosion of historical writing in recent decades, it is almost impossible for a bibliography to list everything on its subject. The works cited are generally not detailed checklists but rather guides to aid researchers in their tasks. What is not found in one bibliography will often be found in another, so researchers may need to use a number of works that by their titles seem to be duplications.

Full bibliographical information for titles is entered only once, and each item is assigned a reference number placed in brackets *before* the title. If cross-references are made, the title is given in short form with the reference number entered *after* the title (so that the reader can quickly locate full information on the work). The author-title-subject index can be used for more thorough cross-referencing. The index generally refers to the bracketed reference numbers, but in appropriate cases pages are cited instead. Citations of works in most cases do not distinguish "author," "editor," or "compiler," but simply indicate the person or persons responsible for the work.

The *Handbook* offers a combination of annotated and unannotated items. The broader and more important works are discussed in the text; more specialized items are generally simply listed, with only brief annotations or none at all. Most readers will be able to decide quickly which of the cited works might be of use to them.

It will be clear to users that the *Handbook* is a guide to sources, not to historical method, for which a number of useful works already exist. In a few cases, however, reference is made to books and articles that offer an introduction to new methods and new subjects.

1

A Revolution in Access to Research Materials

Researchers in American history find themselves in the midst of an ongoing technological revolution. The traditional reliance on paper documents, whether printed or in manuscript form, located through card catalogs or printed bibliographies and reference guides, is giving way to new forms of guides and in some cases to new forms of text.

Microforms

The revolution began with photographic reproduction of materials. There are few students or scholars today who have not long been accustomed to using microfilm, which can reproduce and make widely available sources that would otherwise be hard to acquire. By this means unique manuscripts can be put in the hands of many researchers, and bulky items like daily newspapers that filled the space on many shelves can be stored compactly in cabinet drawers.

Microfilm has not been replaced, but it has been augmented by other forms of photographic reproduction. Opaque cards, large or small, were first used—some of which reproduced materials in reduced form photographically, while others (like Readex Microprint) printed the miniaturized material on the cards. Such cards are more difficult to read than microfilm, and it is hard to copy material from them. Although some libraries still maintain large research collections on opaque cards, that technology has been replaced by reproduction on microfiche, sheets of photographic film which combine the advantages of card format with the ease of reading and of copying of microfilm. Immense amounts of material of use to students of American history have been and continue to be published in microfiche format.

Online Databases

Printing and photographic reproduction are now being replaced by electronic technology, and there may soon come a day, some enthusiasts predict, when paper or photographic film will be obsolete. Massive databases have been digitally recorded and made available in a variety of forms. Most large commercial bibliographies in paper form are now printed from computerized databases, and more and more of this information is available online, that is, the data can be called up on a computer monitor and can be searched by sophisticated techniques using keywords, library call numbers, time frame, language, or geographical place, as well as traditional author, title, and subject headings. The bibliographic databases are updated periodically (sometimes daily), can be used by many patrons at once, and can be accessed from distant terminals (even personal computers). The material on the screen can be immediately printed or can be downloaded into the researcher's own computerized document files.

Most sizable libraries today provide their catalogs online, although large libraries are still working on the tremendous task of producing machine-readable records for their older holdings.

In addition, most libraries subscribe to database services, which provide a great variety of information retrieval programs. Some of the most commonly used vendors are the following:

BRS Information Technologies
DIALOG Information Services
LEXIS (Mead Data Central)
NEXIS (Mead Data Central)
OCLC Online Computer Library Center
OCLC EPIC
OCLC FirstSearch Catalog
WESTLAW (West Publishing Company)
WILSONLINE (H. W. Wilson Company)

To use these online services it is best and often necessary to rely on mediated searches, that is, searches conducted by library personnel after consultation with the researcher. Library specialists know what databases are available in the library and how best to access them. Since the cost of the use of most online databases is determined by the time involved, researchers will not want to waste time in trying to turn up useful data. The computer, it must be remembered, is literal and cannot recognize synonymous terms, nor can it distinguish between the variant meanings of a single term, so many useless citations may turn up while relevant ones are missed.

A movement is gaining force, however, to make online databases directly available to the end-user (that is, the searcher who ultimately uses the data) rather than to depend upon mediated searches by librarians. As researchers become more sophisticated in their knowledge and use of electronic sources, as the interfaces between users and databases are simplified and made more user friendly, and as pricing schemes are changed so that use becomes less costly, the day may arrive when most online facilities can be accessed directly, easily, and perhaps cheaply by the researchers themselves. One step in that direction is to add commercial electronic bibliographies to the library's own regular online catalog, thus enabling researchers, at the library's catalog terminals, to have additional information at their fingertips. Another and very important development now toward end-user accessibility is the use of CD-ROMs, which will be discussed below.

Online databases saw their earliest and greatest development in the sciences and social sciences. Only slowly are databases designed particularly for historians appearing. But many general bibliographic materials online—like periodical and newspaper directories and indexes, biographical guides, and guides to federal government publications—are essential to historical research. If materials are available both in traditional printed form and in online databases, the researcher in American history will have to determine which form is more expeditious for the particular search at hand. Sometimes it is difficult to use electronic databases efficiently without knowing well the paper forms they duplicate or replace.

Historians, moreover, unlike scholars in many other disciplines, are interested as much in old materials as in current ones. That puts them at a disadvantage in regard to the electronic databases, for these new products generally (although not exclusively) provide relatively recent materials. While many library online catalogs now include all the materials in the library, and while some national databases also are retrospective, many of the ongoing computerized bibliographic indexes go back only to the 1970s or 1980s. Some few are beginning to backtrack, in order to cover material retrospectively, but the movement is slow because just keeping up with currently appearing materials is a sizable and expensive task.

Researchers will be dependent upon the library or libraries in which they work for access to online databases, for these institutions supply the workstations and subscribe to selected database services for their patrons. Not all libraries will have all the databases that exist. To see what else might be available, one can use published online database directories, such as [1] *Directory of Online Databases* (Detroit: Gale Research, 1992). This work, begun in the fall of 1979, was originally published quarterly by Cuadra Associates, Santa Monica, California, but now appears semiannually. The July 1992 edition of the directory describes more than 5,300 databases, showing type (bibliographic or full text), publisher, online services from which they are available, content, language, geographical coverage, time span, frequency of updating, and availability of contents in other media. A subject index helps locate databases of interest.

Those who are interested in keeping up with new online offerings and discussions of new technologies will find useful material in [2] *Online: The Magazine of Online Information Systems,* which began publication as a quarterly in 1977 but changed to bimonthly publication in 1982. There exists also an extensive literature of books and articles that describe and discuss techniques of online searching.

The Advent of CD-ROMs

A new entry in the information technology sweepstakes is CD-ROM (Compact Disc—Read Only Memory). This technology has made almost unbelievable advances since it was introduced commercially in 1985.

A CD-ROM is like an audio CD, a small disc, less than five inches in diameter, whose digital data are inscribed and read by a laser beam. What first strikes the user is the remarkable capacity of a single disc. Estimates vary, but in general a single disc can hold about 600 megabytes of data. That is equivalent to 200,000 or more pages of printed material, a million catalog cards, or data from 1,500 floppy discs. The read-only nature of the CD-ROMs, which means that the data on the disc cannot be added to or erased, makes the CD-ROMs like books, articles, and other paper sources. An early analysis of the technology, in fact, spoke of CD-ROMs as the "new papyrus."

The special hardware and software needed to use CD-ROMs, ordinarily supplied by the library, is geared directly to the end-user, although some tutorial help from librarians may be needed to get started, especially since the interfaces on the various discs are not yet uniform and some are more difficult to master than others. Once installed, the CD-ROMs offer a wide variety of search techniques (which vary from producer to producer). The H. W. Wilson Company, which provides CD-ROMs as well as printed and online versions of its periodical indexes, notes that its CD-ROMs offer the following capabilities for search: keyword, Boolean, search statement retention and back referencing, field searching, proximity searching, printing, downloading, truncation, thesaurus, novice search mode, search saving, automatic singular and plural, nesting, and local holdings display. The last is a useful service, for the screen will indicate whether or not the library subscribes to the journal in which the located article is published.

A CD-ROM station can be attached to several drives, so that the researcher can draw upon a number of discs that offer a variety of different databases, but many libraries will have stand-alone stations for heavily used discs. There are developments aimed at networking CD-ROMs to provide multiple access to a drive and the possibility of remote access, but the final stages in these developments still seem some time in the future.

CD-ROMs have been enthusiastically received by users because of their large storage capacity and their direct access by the end-user. Updating, however, requires a new disc, since nothing can be added to an existing one. And, until more retrospective databases are produced on disc, history researchers will find much CD-ROM information too current for many of their needs. Whereas online databases cover material from the 1970s, the CD-ROMs' beginning dates are the mid-1980s or later.

New CD-ROMs are appearing at such a rapid rate that the directories can hardly keep up. The wide array of sources available in all fields can be seen in [3] *CD-ROM Collection Builder's Toolkit,* by Paul T. Nicholls (Weston, Conn.: Eight Bit Books, 1991); [4] *CD-ROM Research Collections: An Evaluative Guide to Bibliographies and Full-Text CD-ROM Databases,* by Pat Ensor (Westport, Conn.: Meckler, 1991); and especially [5] *CD-ROMs in Print,* an annual directory published in Westport, Connecticut, by Meckler since 1987. The 1992 edition, compiled by Norman Desmarais, lists nearly 3,000 titles commercially available. Current developments can be followed in such periodicals as [6] *CD-ROM Professional,* published bimonthly since 1990 by Pemberton Press in Weston, Connecticut, and [7] *CD-ROM Librarian,* published bimonthly since 1987 by Meckler. The latter also prints supplements to *CD-ROMs in Print.*

Full Text

Both online and CD-ROM technology can make available full-text materials. While the history researcher now will find the technologies most useful as bibliographical tools, the offerings in full text are beginning to proliferate. Current legal materials—bills, laws, resolutions, and other such items, the *Congressional Record,* the *Federal Register,* and the *Code of Federal Regulations*—are available online and in some cases also on CD-ROM. Recent United States census data are available. And a considerable number of metropolitan daily newspapers are offered in a full-text version both online and on CD-ROMs. But these materials are generally dated from the mid-1980s or later. Historians will have to wait until more full-text versions of older historical materials are published in digital computerized form.

The Internet

Diverse sources of electronically stored data exist for researchers in local, national, and international networks. Local networks of computers are joined together for larger supernetworks, held together by commonly agreed upon protocols for access to the databases they hold. The most important of these is the Internet, which developed as a network of networks, aided by the National Science Foundation, to enable scientists to communicate rapidly with each other about research projects. The Internet is now used by scholars in all disciplines and serves three functions: it offers a means for electronic mail, by which messages can be sent by members to each other and bulletin boards or conferences dealing with particular areas of research can be communicated; it permits the transfer of files of data from one computer on the network to another; and it allows a person at one computer to use directly databases at other, often distant, computers. The latter function, for example, now provides access to dozens and dozens of online library catalogs in libraries across the United States and around the world. All this is available at little or no cost to researchers who can make use of Internet access through a college or university. The growing popularity of the Internet has spawned a number of instructional manuals with such catchy titles as *Crossing the Internet Threshold, The Internet Companion,* and *Zen and the Art of the Internet.* (A similar but less extensive network that ties many higher educational institutions together is BITNET [Because It's Time Network], and the two networks have some interfacing.)

A new national development that bears watching is the National Research and Education Network (NREN), authorized by the High-Performance Computing Act of 1991, which became law on December 9, 1991 (105 Stat. 1594). Now funded with $2 billion over a five-year period, the network aims to transmit data at one gigabit or more a second by 1996. Although NREN is designed primarily to assist the scientific community and to keep the United States a leader in computer science and technology, humanistic scholars can profit from it as well. The network, the law says, "shall provide for the linkage of research institutions and educational institutions, government, and industry in every State . . . [and] provide access, to the extent practicable, to electronic information resources maintained by libraries, research facilities, publishers, and affiliated organizations." NREN, when operative, will replace many of the functions of the Internet.

How useful these networks are to researchers in American history is difficult at present to assess. They certainly make possible close contact between historians working on similar projects, and for specialized searches access to the catalogs of other libraries may prove of significant value. But the extensive accessibility of large commercial bibliographical databases (online or on CD-ROMs) may make access to a large variety of library catalogs less valuable than it might otherwise be. Historians interested in the networks' possibilities would do well to query college and university computer centers and libraries about the current status of the networks, the directories of databases available on them, and up-to-date guides to their use.

Because bibliographic and other reference works and sources in printed form are still the mainstay for research in American history (and will remain so until electronic databases move more widely toward retrospective not just recent coverage), the *Handbook* centers its attention on printed works, but it notes the availability of the information also in electronic form (online or CD-ROMs). These notations will be quickly out of date, of course, as new electronic sources appear, but updated directories of such materials will enable researchers to locate new databases of interest to them.

2

General Guides to Reference Works

Researchers in American history need to be acquainted with general reference guides, although these works may have only a small section devoted specifically to American history. The most important such publication is [8] *Guide to Reference Books,* by Eugene P. Sheehy, 10th ed. (Chicago: American Library Association, 1986), which is the most recent in a long line of editions of a work that has been a standard tool for many years (earlier editions were edited by I. G. Mudge and by Constance M. Winchell). A supplement to the 10th edition, edited by Robert Balay, covering material from 1985 to 1990, was published in 1992. The *Guide* and the supplement have a section on general reference works as well as one section devoted to United States history; other sections on the humanities and the social sciences describe reference tools that often are useful for historians. The descriptive annotations are brief but trustworthy.

Another broad and useful listing of reference books by subjects is [9] *The Library of Congress Main Reading Room Reference Collection Subject Catalog,* by Katherine Ann Gardner, 2d ed. (Washington: Library of Congress, 1980). This computer-generated list of 1,236 pages contains 17,315 titles, primarily in humanities, social sciences, and bibliography.

For extensive critical reviews of new books year by year, a good source is [10] *American Reference Books Annual (ARBA)*, edited by Bohdan S. Wynar (Littleton, Colo.: Libraries Unlimited, 1970–). This series began in 1970 and has so far been published through 1992. Each volume is arranged by subject categories and has an author-subject-title index; there are cumulative indexes for 1970–1974, 1975–1979, 1980–1984, and 1985–1989. The quarterly periodical [11] *RSR: Reference Services Review,* which began publication in 1973, reviews new reference books in all fields and regularly has bibliographical articles dealing with American history in general or with special aspects of it.

Of special help to beginning researchers in history is a selective guide to all fields of history: [12] *Reference Sources in History: An Introductory Guide,* by Ronald H. Fritze, Brian E. Coutts, and Louis A. Vyhnanek (Santa Barbara, Calif.: ABC-Clio, 1990). It has long descriptions and evaluations of the works cited and includes a good many books for American history, which are often set apart in separate sections within the chapters. It largely supersedes an earlier similar guide: [13] *The Historian's Handbook: A Descriptive Guide to Reference Works,* by Helen J. Poulton (Norman: University of Oklahoma Press, 1972), which also covers all areas of history, not just that of the United States. Another helpful listing is [14] *The Craft of Public History: An Annotated Select Bibliography,* by David F. Trask and Robert W. Pomeroy III (Westport, Conn.: Greenwood Press, 1983), which is more inclusive than its title suggests. A brief introduction to reference guides for American history, with a selected list of 140 titles, classified in 5 broad groups and 23 categories, is [15] "Clio's Neglected Tools: A Taxonomy of Reference Works for American History," by Lawrence B. de Graaf, *History Teacher* 25 (February 1992): 191–231.

Researchers who want a different approach to searching for materials in libraries than that offered in this *Handbook* will find much sage advice and brief descriptions of a large number of reference guides and bibliographies in [16] *A Guide to Library Research Methods,* by Thomas Mann (New York: Oxford University Press, 1987). The author has been a general reference librarian at the Library of Congress and has had other broad library experience, and he draws as well on methods he has observed in other researchers. He provides excellent discussions, for example, of subject headings in catalogs, use of keyword searches, systematic browsing, and computer searches.

A researcher can keep up to date on history reference publications by scanning the recent publications listed in the "Documents and Bibliographies" section of each issue of the [17] *American Historical Review,* which lists United States items in a separate part, and in the [18] *Journal of American History,* which lists periodical articles and dissertations in its "Recent Scholarship" section under the heading "Archives and Bibliography." The *Journal* since 1987 has also published annually in its March issue a section on "Research and Reference Tools: Reviews," which provides information on recent reference books. A semiannual publication of the Association for the Bibliography of History, the [19] *ABH Bulletin,* reports on new history bibliographical materials and projects. A recent series, appearing annually, is [20] *American History: A Bibliographic Review,* edited by Carol Bondhus Fitzgerald (Westport, Conn.: Meckler Publishing, 1985–). It publishes articles on bibliographical subjects of interest to American historians, special bibliographies, and reviews of pertinent reference books.

3

Libraries: Catalogs and Guides

The workshop of the historical researcher is the library, and researchers quickly find a home in the local university or public library. The library's catalogs and other finding aids are often the first resort in looking for materials on a research topic. Most libraries, even though few if any can supply all the sources one needs, are well equipped with reference books and guides, and many subscribe to the electronic databases that replace or augment printed works.

Library Catalogs

Library catalogs are a great resource, even though they do not offer a critically selected list of works and do not furnish annotations. They show the works in a given library, good books as well as old or useless ones, and in most cases they do not indicate articles in periodicals. But they cannot be neglected, and those of large research libraries and those that are union catalogs furnish a wealth of information.

Libraries in recent years have undergone a revolution in line with the high tech society that they serve. Some, of course, still maintain a traditional card catalog with its hundreds of drawers of 3 x 5 cards, now often broken down into separate title, author, and subject catalogs. Other libraries have closed their card catalogs at a specific date, and materials cataloged subsequent to the closing date must be searched for in electronic databases through computer terminals. Some of the closed card catalogs have physically disappeared, the cards having been reproduced in bound printed volumes available in multiple copies for researchers' use. Many libraries have put *all* their catalog data into a retrospective database, to which access is gained through terminals. Serials collections, too, have been computerized, and computer-generated microforms or huge printouts of them are often available unless the data have been entered into the libraries' online catalogs.

The move toward electronic libraries is sure to continue until, in the vision of some librarians, printed matter will all but disappear or be placed in storage, while the library patrons sit at workstations that can call up the full text of books and articles as well as a variety of bibliographic databases. But an argument goes on between those who see the librarians' function still as developing collections and those who think that collections on hand are less important than electronic access to materials no matter where they exist.

The history researcher for the present and into the indefinite future, however, will need to rely heavily on traditional printed or microform materials, since the new electronic access tools, as we have seen, are useful for current or recent materials, not for the older materials that historians are most likely to need. And they are heavily weighted toward science, technology, business, and social science, not toward history.

National Libraries

A researcher must often go beyond local libraries and exploit the resources of great libraries that serve the whole nation, such as the Library of Congress and the New York Public Library. It is not necessary any longer to go to these institutions to discover what they hold, for their catalogs, all or in part, have been reproduced in printed books or by electronic means and are available in libraries throughout the nation.

The Library of Congress is the premier library of the United States, and its printed catalogs for a long time were a mainstay in library cataloging departments, although history students often neglect them. Sometimes, in fact, they are hidden away in the technical services division of the library and are all but inaccessible to library patrons unless they are insistently sought out. Of great importance is the fact that the more recent Library of Congress author catalogs are *union catalogs,* that is, in addition to the holdings of the Library of Congress they report items in other participating libraries so that the number of publications listed is tremendously increased.

Printed catalogs of the Library of Congress in book form have appeared since the mid-1940s, in a confusing series of sets, with some overlapping and bewildering changes in titles. Many of these early sets of multiple volumes, however, are no longer needed by the historical researcher, for new publications have cumulated the older information.

The researcher who wants information in printed form can usually begin with [21] *The National Union Catalog: Pre-1956 Imprints,* 754 vols. (London: Mansell Information/Publishing, 1968–1981). This huge set of oversize volumes, often referred to simply as "Mansell," is a cumulative author list representing Library of Congress printed cards plus titles reported by several hundred other American libraries. Volumes 686–754 are a *Supplement* with a new alphabetical listing. With respect to Library of Congress holdings, this series replaces earlier sets of author catalogs.

For post-1956 imprints, a successive series of volumes must be used. One of these is [22] *The National Union Catalog: A Cumulative Author List, 1958–1962,* 52 vols. (New York: Rowman and Littlefield, 1963). This set, as well as earlier series, is included in a cumulative series published as a private commercial venture: [23] *Library of Congress and National Union Catalog Author Lists, 1942–1962: A Master Cumulation,* 152 vols. (Detroit: Gale Research Company, 1969–1971). See also [24] *The National Union Catalog, 1956 through 1967: A Cumulative Author List Representing Library of Congress Printed Cards and Titles Reported by Other American Libraries,* 125 vols. (Totowa, N.J.: Rowman and Littlefield, 1970–1972).

After 1962 the following multivolume sets continue the National Union Catalog author lists:

[25] *The National Union Catalog: A Cumulative Author List, 1963–1967,* 67 vols. (Ann Arbor: J. W. Edwards, 1969). Vols 60–67 are a [26] *Register of Additional Locations,* which notes locations of works not shown earlier.

[27] *The National Union Catalog: A Cumulative Author List, 1968–1972,* 119 vols. (Ann Arbor: J. W. Edwards, 1973). Vols. 105–119 are the *Register of Additional Locations.*

[28] *National Union Catalog, 1973–1977,* 135 vols. (Totowa, N.J.: Rowman and Littlefield, 1978).

These are followed by annual multivolume sets published by the Library of Congress from 1978 to 1982. Beginning in 1972 the [29] *National Union Catalog: Register of Additional Locations* appeared as a separate series in annual sets of 2–4 volumes. By 1991 the *Register of Additional Locations* included more than 40 million locations, with about half a million new location symbols added each year.

The author listings in the *National Union Catalog* are useful in many ways to researchers in American history topics, but of greater help in accumulating titles of useful works on a given subject are the Library of Congress printed subject catalogs, which started in 1950. At first called [30] *Library of Congress Catalog, Books: Subjects,* after 1975 the series used the simple title [31] *Subject Catalog.*

The Library of Congress beginning in 1974 also published a [32] *Monographic Series* in annual sets of 3–5 volumes. These catalogs compiled Library of Congress printed catalog cards representing all monographs cataloged by the library as parts of series.

After the 1982 issues, the Library of Congress published no more printed catalogs in book form, using instead computerized catalogs issued in microfiche form. The one that researchers in United States history will need to use is [33] *National Union Catalog: Books,* which represents the works cataloged by the Library of Congress and by about 1,100 contributing libraries. It supersedes the *National Union Catalog,* the *Subject Catalog,* and the *Monographic Series,* formerly published in book form.

The *National Union Catalog: Books* has a *Register,* which includes full bibliographic information on a book; items are arranged in numerical order, with a register number assigned to each in sequence; there are four indexes, which provide limited information but refer the user to the corresponding register number, so that full information can be sought in the *Register* if it is needed. The indexes are (1) *Name Index,* which provides access to all names and name-title combinations used as main or added entry items; (2) *Title Index,* a new service; (3) *LC Subject Index*; and (4) *LC Series Index.* The *Register* is a permanent file of microfiche, with additional register numbers added monthly. The indexes are periodically updated; the new indexes supersede the previous ones, which are then discarded. Beginning in 1990, however, the Library of Congress no longer includes in the *National Union Catalog* as many entries supplied by other libraries as it once did. It no longer accepts items if the libraries holding them have submitted them to the Online Computer Library Catalog (OCLC), the Research Libraries Information Network (RLIN), or the Western Library Network (WLN). What remains are Library of Congress cataloging, reports for books from United States libraries that create records for local systems, reports from Canadian libraries, reports of microform masters, and reports from other libraries that do not contribute to OCLC, RLIN, or WLN. The frequency of publication and the microfiche format remain the same.

Historians will also be interested in the Library of Congress's [34]

National Union Catalog: Cartographic Materials, which is available in a microfiche *Register.* It contains bibliographic records of single maps, sets of maps, and atlases cataloged by the Library of Congress and records of atlases contributed by 1,500 other libraries. In 1983 the entire retrospective Library of Congress maps database was added, and there are annual supplements.

Another Library of Congress catalog of interest to historians is [35] *Catalog of Broadsides in the Rare Book Division,* 4 vols. (Boston: G. K. Hall and Company, 1972), which provides a geographical shelflist catalog, an author and title catalog, and a chronological catalog.

To use the Library of Congress catalogs effectively—and those, too, of other libraries and bibliographic services that use the Library of Congress subject headings—it is necessary to refer to [36] *Library of Congress Subject Headings* (Washington: Library of Congress), now in its 15th ed., 1992, comprising 4 volumes. These volumes provide an alphabetical listing of subjects used in cataloging at the Library of Congress since 1898. They indicate by cross-references when necessary the precise heading used by the Library of Congress. New subject headings are added and old ones revised, now on an annual basis. In the 15th edition approximately 192,000 headings appear, and from 5,000 to 7,000 more are added each year.

In 1968 the Library of Congress began cataloging its materials in MARC (MAchine-Readable Cataloging) format, which makes possible electronic searching of the Library of Congress catalogs from that date on. MARC records are held by the large bibliographic utilities and can be accessed through their online databases (see discussion below). And the Library of Congress itself makes available its machine-readable records on tapes or on CD-ROM. The files most useful for researchers in history will likely be [37] *LC MARC: Books All,* which corresponds to the *National Union Catalog* from 1968 to date; it is available online and on CD-ROM. Other Library of Congress MARC services provide records for maps, music, serials, and visual materials.

The second largest library in the United States is the New York Public Library. For its research collections there is a printed catalog: [38] *Dictionary Catalog of the Research Libraries of the New York Public Library, 1911–1971,* 800 vols. (New York: New York Public Library; printed and distributed, Boston: G. K. Hall Company, 1979). In its 800 volumes are 435,507 pages, with reproduction of over 9 million cards. For items cataloged since 1971 users of the library can use a special computer catalog, called C A T N Y P (Catalog of the New York Public Library), but printed catalogs, also, have been published: [39] *Dictionary Catalog of the Research Libraries: A Cumulative List of Authors, Titles, and Subjects Representing Books and Book-Like Materials Added to the Collections since January 1, 1971* (New York: New York Public Library, 1972); cumulations for 1972–1980 (64 vols.) and for 1981–1988 (73 vols.) were published in 1980 and 1988.

It is unlikely that many libraries will purchase the 800-volume *Dictionary Catalog* and the supplements, but there are earlier publications of catalogs of special collections in the New York Public Library, which are more widely available. Some of them include material that is not part of the 800-volume *Dictionary Catalog*.

One catalog of special importance to researchers in United States history is the [40] *Dictionary Catalog of the History of the Americas,* 28 vols. (Boston: G. K. Hall and Company, 1961), with a supplement of 9 vols. published in 1974. This is the catalog of the library's American History Room and covers both South and North America. In addition to the books it catalogs, it includes many subject cards for periodical articles indexed by the library. Other printed catalogs of the New York Public Library that may be of use are the following:

[41] *Subject Catalog of the World War I Collection,* 4 vols. (Boston: G. K. Hall and Company, 1961).

[42] *Subject Catalog of the World War II Collection,* 3 vols. (Boston: G. K. Hall and Company, 1977).

[43] *Dictionary Catalog of the Map Division,* 10 vols. (Boston: G. K. Hall and Company, 1971), which is supplemented by *Bibliographic Guide to Maps and Atlases* [52].

[44] *Dictionary Catalog of the Schomburg Collection of Negro Literature and History,* 9 vols. (Boston: G. K. Hall and Company, 1962). Supplements were issued in 1967 (4 vols.), 1972 (4 vols.), and 1976 (1 vol.). Additional supplements appear in *Bibliographic Guide to Black Studies* [51].

[45] *Dictionary Catalog of the Local History and Genealogy Division,* 18 vols. (Boston: G. K. Hall and Company, 1974). A selection from this catalog has been issued as [46] *United States Local History Catalog,* 2 vols., 1974.

[47] *Dictionary Catalog of Materials on New York City,* 3 vols. (Boston: G. K. Hall and Company, 1977).

[48] *Guide to Festschriften,* 2 vols. (Boston: G. K. Hall and Company, 1977). Volume 2 includes items also from the Library of Congress (1968–1976).

[49] *Dictionary Catalog of the Rare Book Division,* 21 vols. (Boston: G. K. Hall and Company, 1971).

A helpful general guide is [50] *Guide to the Research Collections of the New York Public Library,* by Sam P. Williams (Chicago: American Library Association, 1975).

A number of the printed catalogs of the Library of Congress and the New York Public Library have been and continue to be updated by series of annual volumes published by G. K. Hall and Company that list all the works on given topics cataloged by the Library of Congress and the New York Public Library (and other libraries as well) in a given year. The series covers 23 major areas, of which the following may be of use to researchers in American history:

[51] *Bibliographic Guide to Black Studies,* a supplement to the *Dictionary Catalog of the Schomburg Collection of Negro Literature and History* [44]

[52] *Bibliographic Guide to Maps and Atlases,* a supplement to *Dictionary Catalog of the Map Division* [43].

[53] *Bibliographic Guide to Microform Publications,* which provides some information formerly found in the *National Register of Microfilm Masters* [152], discontinued in 1983.

[54] *Bibliographic Guide to North American History,* which supplements the *Dictionary Catalog of the History of the Americas* [40] and the *United States Local History Catalog* [46].

[55] *Bibliographic Guide to Education,* which supplements the *Dictionary Catalog of the Teachers College Library* [79].

Special Library Catalogs

Most researchers will sooner or later come in contact with specialized libraries dealing with particular aspects of American history, such as the library of the State Historical Society of Wisconsin in Madison, the Newberry Library in Chicago, the Henry E. Huntington Library in San Marino, California, the John Carter Brown Library at Brown University in Providence, Rhode Island, and the William L. Clements Library at the University of Michigan in Ann Arbor. They have brief printed guides to their collections, and for some of them printed catalogs of the holdings or of special collections are available. A very useful guide to such publications is [56] *A Guide to Published Library Catalogs,* by Bonnie R. Nelson (Metuchen, N.J.: Scarecrow Press, 1982), which has an exhaustive list of printed catalogs, including those of the Library of Congress and the New York Public Library, and which provides extensive descriptive annotations. A somewhat similar work is [57] *Published Library Catalogues: An Introduction to Their Contents and Use,* by Robert Collison (London: Mansell Information/Publishing, 1973).

The following catalogs should be noted; they are arranged alphabetically by repository.

[58] *A Dictionary Catalog of American Books Pertaining to the 17th through 19th Centuries,* Library of the American Antiquarian Society, 20 vols. (Westport, Conn.: Greenwood Publishing Corporation, 1971).

[59] *Research Catalogue of the American Geographical Society,* 15 vols. (Boston: G. K. Hall and Company, 1962). Vols. 1–2 are a general topical catalog; the remaining volumes are regional, with vols. 4–5 devoted to the United States. Supplements of 2 vols. each were issued in 1972, 1974, and 1978, divided into topical and regional volumes.

[60] *Catalog of Books in the American Philosophical Society Library, Philadelphia, Pennsylvania,* 28 vols. (Westport, Conn.: Greenwood Press, 1970).

[61] *Author-Title Catalog of the Baker Library,* 22 vols. (Boston: G. K. Hall and Company, 1971), and *Subject Catalog of the Baker Library,* 10 vols. (Boston: G. K. Hall and Company, 1971). The Baker Library of the Harvard University Graduate School of Business Administration is a major research library for material in business and economics. The author-title catalog has a supplement of 2 vols. (1974), and the subject catalog has a supplement of 1 vol. (1974).

[62] *Catalog of Printed Books,* Bancroft Library, University of California, Berkeley, 22 vols. (Boston: G. K. Hall and Company, 1964). There were supplements of 6 vols. each in 1969 and 1974 and of 5 vols. in 1979.

[63] *Author-Title Catalog of the William Wyles Collection,* University of California, Santa Barbara, Library, 3 vols. (Westport, Conn.: Greenwood Publishing Corporation, 1970), to which is added *Subject Catalog of the William Wyles Collection,* 2 vols. The collection

deals with Lincoln, the Civil War, and American westward expansion.

[64] *The Center for Research Libraries Catalogue,* microfiche (Chicago: Center for Research Libraries, 1982). Microfiche supplements have been issued through 1989. See also [65] *The Center for Research Libraries Handbook* (Chicago: Center for Research Libraries, 1990), which provides an overview of all the collections of the Center.

[66] *Author/Title Catalog of Americana, 1493–1860, in the William L. Clements Library, University of Michigan,* 5 vols. (Boston: G. K. Hall and Company, 1970), to which is added vols. 6 and 7, [67] *Chronological Catalog of Americana, 1493–1860* (1970).

[68] *Catalog of the Western History Department,* Denver Public Library, 7 vols. (Boston: G. K. Hall and Company, 1970). A supplement appeared in 1975.

[69] *Dictionary Catalog of the Negro Collection of the Fisk University Library,* Nashville, 6 vols. (Boston: G. K. Hall and Company, 1974).

[70] *Catalog of the Foreign Relations Library,* New York, 9 vols. (Boston: G. K. Hall and Company, 1969). A supplement of 3 vols. was published in 1980.

[71] *Catalog of the Friends Historical Library Book and Serial Collections,* Swarthmore College, 6 vols. (Boston: G. K. Hall and Company, 1982).

[72] *Dictionary Catalog of the Hawaiian Collection,* University of Hawaii Library, 4 vols. (Boston: G. K. Hall and Company, 1963).

[73] *The Mereness Calendar: Federal Documents on the Upper Mississippi Valley, 1780–1890,* Illinois Historical Survey, University of Illinois Library, 13 vols. (Boston: G. K. Hall and Company, 1971).

[74] *The Mariners Museum, Newport News, Virginia: Dictionary Catalog of the Library,* 9 vols. (Boston: G. K. Hall and Company, 1964).

[75] *Dictionary Catalog of the Missionary Research Library,* New York, 17 vols. (Boston: G. K. Hall and Company, 1968).

[76] *Dictionary Catalog of the Jesse E. Moorland Collection of Negro Life and History,* Howard University, 9 vols. (Boston: G. K. Hall and Company, 1970). A supplement of 3 vols. was issued in 1976.

[77] *Dictionary Catalog of the Edward E. Ayer Collection of Americana and American Indians in the Newberry Library,* 16 vols. (Boston: G. K. Hall and Company, 1961). A supplement of 3 vols. was issued in 1970 and one of 4 vols. in 1980.

[78] *Library Catalog of the Martin P. Catherwood Library of the New York State School of Industrial and Labor Relations,* Cornell University, 12 vols. (Boston: G. K. Hall and Company, 1967). A cumulated supplement of 9 vols. was issued in 1976, and five supplements to the cumulation have been published, 1977–1982.

[79] *Dictionary Catalog of the Teachers College Library,* Columbia University, 36 vols. (Boston: G. K. Hall and Company, 1970). Three supplements, totaling 17 vols., were issued 1971–1977. Continued by the *Bibliographic Guide to Education* [55].

[80] *Catalog of the Texas Collection in the Barker Texas History Center,* University of Texas at Austin, 14 vols. (Boston: G. K. Hall and Company, 1979).

[81] *Dictionary Catalog of the Pacific Northwest Collection of the University of Washington Libraries, Seattle,* 6 vols. (Boston: G. K. Hall and Company, 1972).

[82] *Author-Title Catalog, Including the City Directory Catalog, Atlas Catalog (Publishers), Atlas Catalog (Geographic), Newspaper Catalog, and Newspaper Catalog (Labor),* State Historical Society of Wisconsin, 22 vols. on 600 sheets of microfiche (Westport, Conn.: Greenwood Publishing Corporation, 1974).

[83] *Subject Catalog of the Library of the State Historical Society of Wisconsin,* 23 vols. (Westport, Conn.: Greenwood Publishing Corporation, 1971).

[84] *Catalog of the Yale Collection of Western Americana,* 4 vols. (Boston: G. K. Hall and Company, 1961). The fourth volume is a shelf-list.

[85] *Catalog of the P. K. Yonge Library of Florida History,* University of Florida, Gainesville, 4 vols. (Boston: G. K. Hall and Company, 1977).

The libraries of the various executive departments of the United States Government have extensive holdings pertinent to their special interests and have useful reference collections and large holdings in federal documents. The rationale for the libraries is to provide reference and source material of use to the departments' personnel, but the libraries are also open to outside scholars. Printed catalogs of some of these libraries were published in the 1960s and 1970s.

[86] *Dictionary Catalog of the National Agricultural Library, 1862–1965,* 73 vols. (New York: Rowman and Littlefield, 1967–1970).

This is continued by a supplement of 12 vols. for the period 1966–1970 (1972–1973).

[87] *Author/Title Catalog of the Department Library,* Department of Health, Education, and Welfare, 29 vols. (Boston, G. K. Hall and Company, 1965). A supplement of 7 vols. was issued in 1973.

[88] *Subject Catalog of the Department Library,* Department of Health, Education, and Welfare, 20 vols. (Boston: G. K. Hall and Company, 1965). A supplement of 4 vols. was issued in 1973.

[89] *Dictionary Catalog of the United States Department of Housing and Urban Development Library and Information Division,* 19 vols. (Boston: G. K. Hall and Company, 1972). Supplements of 2 vols. each were published in 1974 and 1975.

[90] *Dictionary Catalog of the Department Library,* Department of the Interior, 37 vols. (Boston: G. K. Hall and Company, 1967). Four supplements, totaling 18 vols., were issued 1968–1975.

[91] *United States Department of Labor Library Catalog,* 38 vols. (Boston: G. K. Hall and Company, 1975).

Most of the printed library catalogs that are noted in this chapter are products of the 1960s and 1970s. Although a good number have multi-volume supplements, the publishing of such massive catalogs all but stopped by the late 1970s as other means of access to the library holdings, chiefly online databases, were introduced. The G. K. Hall items, if now out of print, are still available for purchase on microfilm.

National Online Library Catalogs

The development of online bibliographic databases has greatly affected library catalog searches. No longer is it necessary to rely solely on the catalogs (card or electronic) of one's local libraries or on printed catalogs of the Library of Congress, the New York Public Library, and other libraries. Many of the functions of these catalogs have been taken over increasingly by massive union catalog databases produced and serviced by special institutions or organizations. The two most important databases are those of the OCLC Online Computer Library Center, located at Dublin, Ohio, and the Research Libraries Group (RLG).

The OCLC Online Computer Library Center began as a means of resource sharing among libraries. By providing cataloging information to member libraries, it reduced the per unit cost of cataloging for libraries and also increased the availability of library resources to users of the libraries. It was also a major resource for interlibrary loan departments. As of 1992 the OCLC Online Union Catalog, containing records from the Library of Congress and from its thousands of member libraries, had an estimated 24 million records. For many years after its beginning as the Ohio College Library Center in 1971, OCLC was used primarily by librarians and was all but inaccessible to library patrons, nor did it serve researchers well, for it was not geared to searches by subject.

Now that has changed, and the OCLC Online Union Catalog is becoming increasingly accessible, in part because library users are better acquainted with online searching, but more especially because the Online Computer Library Center has developed two new programs. One is called EPIC, a new command-driven full online service with sophisticated searching features, including subject searches, intended for librarians and other experienced users. The other, designed for end-users, is FirstSearch, which contains the database materials found in EPIC or subsets of them but has a menu interface that nonspecialists find easy to use. Both EPIC and FirstSearch make available the full OCLC Online Union Catalog (called WorldCat in FirstSearch), but they also function as online database services, offering their users a wide array of other databases. FirstSearch also provides access to serials information through OCLC/FaxonFinder databases, which supply serials table-of-contents information and provide a document supply service through which users can obtain copies of articles they want. FirstSearch is innovative in its pricing system. Instead of charges determined by the amount of time the database is used, FirstSearch operates (at least now) on a flat charge per completed search, and libraries can buy blocks of searches, which they can use themselves or distribute (free or at cost) among faculty and students. Pricing arrangements, however, are bound to change as market conditions change. Researchers interested in where OCLC is headed can read [92] *Journey to the 21st Century: A Summary of OCLC's Strategic Plan* (Dublin, Ohio: OCLC, 1991).

The Research Libraries Group was created in 1974 to serve the needs of large research libraries and other specialized libraries. It developed a massive online database called RLIN (Research Libraries Information Network), estimated at about 50 million items in 1992, representing the holdings of more than 100 research libraries and archival repositories. RLIN serves its members in much the same way as OCLC does its. Then in 1989 RLIN became available directly to private users through the Internet or through the GTE/Telenet public network, with a set fee for a specified length of connect time. RLIN holds a good many specialized research collections in addition to its basic bibliographic database; the search features are similar to other online databases. In 1992 RLIN introduced a citation and document delivery service called CitaDel and has begun to add commercial databases.

The Internet, besides providing access to RLIN, also gives a researcher the opportunity to use directly the online library catalogs of scores of university libraries. But the large libraries, like Harvard's or Yale's, do not yet have their full library holdings in the machine-readable databases. In October 1992, for example, Harvard University announced an 8-year, $20 million project to convert the remainder of its paper bibliographic records to machine-readable form, an estimated 5 million monograph and serial titles, or about two-thirds of its holdings.

Shelflists

Libraries have traditionally maintained shelflist catalogs, which file items according to call numbers. Researchers may have occasion to use shelflists and should inquire about them in libraries used.

The [93] *Shelflist of the Library of Congress,* now somewhat outdated, is available in microfilm (about 248 reels) from United States Historical Documents Institute, Arlington, Virginia, and in microfilm or microfiche (about 3,229 sheets) from University Microfilms International, Ann Arbor, Michigan. There are two special guides to these lists: [94] *User's Guide to the Library of Congress Shelflist Reference System,* by Nancy Olson (Arlington, Va.: United States Historical Documents Institute, 1980), and [95] *The Library of Congress Shelflist: A User's Guide to the Microfiche Edition,* by Linda K. Hamilton, 2 vols. (Ann Arbor, Mich.: University Microfilms International, 1979).

If a library has an up-to-date electronic catalog of its holdings that allows searches by call number, it no longer needs to maintain a separate shelflist catalog. Users can move backward and forward under call numbers and thus review the library holdings in the order in which they appear on the shelves.

Guides to Special Libraries and Collections

A number of guides and directories list and classify special libraries, geographically and by subject. These may help a researcher looking for material on particular topics or for resources in a given locality or region. The [96] *Directory of Special Libraries and Information Centers,* by Debra M. Kirby, 16th ed., 1993, 1 vol. in 2 parts (Detroit: Gale Research Inc., 1992), lists libraries alphabetically but includes a subject index. Volume 2, available separately, is entitled [97] *Geographic and Personnel Indexes.* A directory to collections by subject matter is [98] *Subject Collections: A Guide to Special Book Collections and Subject Emphases as Reported by University, College, Public, and Special Libraries and Museums in the United States and Canada,* by Lee Ash and William G. Miller, 6th ed., rev. and enl., 2 vols. (New York: R. R. Bowker Company, 1985). A related and useful work is [99] *Research Centers Directory,* 17th ed., 1993, by Annette Piccirelli (Detroit: Gale Research, 1993), which is a guide to nearly 13,000 research organizations, arranged in 17 sections by field. See section 14, "Humanities and Religion," which includes history.

Other guides to special library collections are the following:

[100] *American Library Resources: A Bibliographical Guide,* by Robert B. Downs (Chicago: American Library Association, 1951). There are supplements for 1950–1961 (1962), 1961–1970 (1972), and 1971–1980 (1981). A cumulative index, 1870–1970, by Clara D. Keller, was published in 1981.

[101] *Special Collections in College and University Libraries,* compiled by Modoc Press, with an introduction by Leona Rostenberg and Madeleine B. Stern (New York: Macmillan Company, 1989). It describes collections at 1,805 institutions, arranged alphabetically by state then by institution.

[102] *Special Collections in the Library of Congress: A Selective Guide,* by Annette Melville (Washington: Library of Congress, 1980).

[103] *A Guide to Special Collections in the OCLC Database,* by Philip Schieber, Virginia G. Voedisch, and Becky A. Wright (Dublin, Ohio: OCLC Online Computer Library Center, 1988).

[104] *Ethnic Collections in Libraries,* by E. J. Josey and Marva L. DeLoach (New York: Neal-Schuman Publishers, 1983).

4

General Bibliographies

Expert bibliographers—a great army of them—have prepared the way for researchers in United States history. They are persons with special skills, who have searched out, classified, listed, and often annotated published books and articles. Their works range from bibliographies of bibliographies to very specialized lists on small topics or of particular kinds of publications. There is no excuse for floundering, wondering what there is on a given subject, when innumerable guides are available. Broader works that list various kinds of materials are considered here, although some examples of more specific bibliographic reference works are added in order to show the variety of materials.

General Bibliographies of American History

Some extensive bibliographies provide classified listings of both books and articles dealing with American history. They are usually the best place to begin preparing a working bibliography on one's specific research topic.

The most important of these, though somewhat confusing to use because of its many distinct parts, is [105] *Writings on American History,* a multivolume work that over the years has had a variety of compilers and publishers; volumes for 1948–1960 were edited by James R. Masterson under the sponsorship of the National Historical Publications Commission and published by the Government Printing Office, 1952–1972. The first stage in the history of the series consisted of annual volumes (generally) for the years 1902 to 1960, with no volumes for 1904–1905 or 1941–1947. Through 1935 the bibliographies included all books and articles, wherever published, which dealt with the history of the United States and British North America and all books published in the United States or Europe on Latin America and the Pacific Islands. Beginning with 1936, publications on Canada and Latin America were omitted unless they concerned diplomatic relations with the United States. The volumes have a classified arrangement, with detailed author-title-subject indexes. Each item in a volume is assigned a serial number, and many entries have brief annotations. For the early volumes there is an [106] *Index to the Writings on American History, 1902–1940* (Washington: American Historical Association, 1956), which directs the user to the annual volumes and the serial numbers of the pertinent items in each.

After the publication of the volume for 1960, there was some delay in continuing this important series. Eventually a new series was begun, and volumes were issued to fill in gaps. The new stage in the history of the *Writings on American History* consists of the following publications.

[107] *Writings on American History, 1961*, compiled by James R. Masterson and Joyce E. Eberly for the National Historical Publications and Records Commission, 2 vols. (Millwood, N.Y.: KTO Press, 1978). This follows the plan of the original series, covering both books and articles.

[108] *Writings on American History, 1962–73: A Subject Bibliography of Articles,* James J. Dougherty, compiler-editor, 4 vols. (Washington: American Historical Association; and Millwood, N.Y.: KTO Press, 1976). Volume 1 contains items arranged by chronological periods, volume 2 by geographical regions, and volumes 3–4 by subjects. There is an author index in volume 4.

[109] *Writings on American History, 1962–73: A Subject Bibliography of Books and Monographs,* based on a compilation by James R. Masterson, 10 vols. (Washington: American Historical Association; and White Plains, N.Y.: Kraus International Publications, 1985). Items are arranged by chronological periods, subject categories, and geographical regions. There are also sections on history and historians and on biography.

For the period after 1973 a new annual series was begun: [110] *Writings on American History: A Subject Bibliography of Articles* (Washington: American Historical Association; and Millwood, N.Y.: Kraus-Thompson Organization, 1974–). Editors have changed over the years, and there are variations in the publisher's designation. The first volume, for 1973–1974, simply used the United States items from the "Recently Published Articles" section of the *American Historical Review*. The series was expanded in subsequent years to include items besides those in "Recently Published Articles," but it still did not include books or monographs. It has convenient subject categories and an author index. The series ended with a volume for 1989–1990.

Writings on American History thus provides a nearly complete listing of books and articles from 1902 to 1973 (with the early gap and the gap from 1941 to 1947 still not filled) and a continuing series from 1973 to 1990 with periodical articles only. It is a major resource, made available by many different bibliographers, organizations, and publishers, public and private. The richness of the whole series can be appreciated only by actual use.

A publication that now continues most of the functions performed by *Writings on American History* is [111] *America: History and Life (AHL)* (Santa Barbara, Calif.: ABC-Clio, 1965–). Originally designed to offer abstracts of periodical literature (it carried the subtitle *Guide to Periodical Literature*), *AHL* expanded to cover citations to book reviews (thus effectively providing a bibliography of new books) and lists of dissertations. It covers the United States and Canada, while a sister publication, *Historical Abstracts,* covers the rest of the world. For some years, *AHL* was published in four parts: Part A, three times a year, provided abstracts arranged by subject (with author, subject, and title indexes); Part B, twice a year, listed book reviews; Part C provided an annual American history bibliography that cited articles in A, reviews in B, and dissertations; and Part D, an annual index. There are five-year indexes for 1964–1969, 1969–1973, 1974–1978 and *Supplement* 1964–1973, 1979–1983, and 1984–1988. The periodical abstracts, done by a corps of volunteers throughout the country, are objective and helpful and now draw articles from more than 2,000 periodicals.

For articles missed by the early volumes, when fewer publications were surveyed for pertinent articles, see [112] *America: History and Life, Supplement to Volumes 1–10,* 2 vols. (Santa Barbara, Calif.: ABC-Clio, 1980), which abstracts and indexes 8,744 articles. There is also a retrospective volume, Volume 0, published in 1972, which contains 6,154 abstracts for the years 1954–1963 taken from *Historical Abstracts,* which beginning with the advent of *AHL* in 1964 no longer included United States and Canadian items.

In 1989 the presentation of material in *America: History and Life* was reorganized, making the work much easier to use. The old Parts A, B, C, and D were replaced by five issues each year, four of which contain periodical abstracts, book review citations, and lists of dissertations under each of the subject headings into which the work is divided; a fifth issue contains a full annual index. The detailed subject indexing of the Subject Profile Index system (SPIndex) provides multiple access to the items. *AHL,* from 1964 to the present, can be searched online through DIALOG and beginning with 1987, on CD-ROM.

The publisher of *America: History and Life* has used the database of that work to produce separately published subject bibliographies, which extract citations and abstracts from the master electronic file. There are more than thirty such bibliographies of use to American historians, ranging in subject matter from women, African Americans, and American Indians to the Constitution, labor, religion, and the family. Some of them are listed in the 1992 *Supplement* to *Guide to Reference Books* [8] in number DA55; others appear in the topical lists in the first edition of this [113] *Handbook for Research in American History* (Lincoln: University of Nebraska Press, 1987). These volumes contain abstracts of periodical articles only, often cover a limited chronological period of publication, and are not up to date. The material they present can be obtained from the printed volumes of *America: History and Life* or from online searches of that database. Yet, it is sometimes convenient to have material on a given subject pulled together, thus reducing the task of drawing up a complete bibliography oneself.

Less up to date than *Writings on American History* and *America: History and Life* but more convenient to use is [114] *Harvard Guide to American History,* rev. ed., edited by Frank Freidel, 2 vols. (Cambridge: Harvard University Press, 1974), which largely, but not completely, replaces an earlier edition of 1954 edited by Oscar Handlin and others. Volume 1 includes essays on research methods and materials and provides lists of books and articles arranged by topics; volume 2 is arranged according to chronological periods. There is a lengthy index of names and a shorter subject index. The entries are given in somewhat abbreviated form, but the *Guide* contains a wealth of material, and it can get a researcher started on just about any topic related to the history of the United States.

Convenient selected bibliographies on various aspects of American history appear in the 22-volume series [115] *Goldentree Bibliographies in American History,* under the general editorship of Arthur S. Link, published first by Appleton-Century-Croft and then by AHM Publishing Corporation. They cover both chronological periods and special topics. They have not been updated, but taken together they offer a reasonably complete bibliography, prepared by knowledgeable historians, on American history up to their dates of publication. A complete list of them with publication data is given in the first edition of this *Handbook* [113].

Beginning in 1957 the American Historical Association, through its Service Center for Teachers of History, published a series of [116] *AHA Pamphlets,* which are brief historiographical and bibliographical essays by noted scholars. There are more than 75 pamphlets, on a variety of historical topics, including a large number in United States history. Although a few have been updated in revised editions, most are now out of date; nevertheless, they provide useful introductions to significant older writings and to historical interpretations.

A useful publication, not so much for intensive research as for finding general background materials on a broad variety of American history topics, is [117] *A Guide to the Study of the United States of America: Representative Books Reflecting the Development of American Life and Thought* (Washington: Library of Congress, 1960). Prepared under the direction of Roy P. Basler by Donald H. Mugridge and Blanche P. Mc-Crum, the large volume provides brief informative reviews of the books included. A *Supplement, 1956–1965,* following the same pattern, was published in 1976.

A very general introductory guide to American history research is [118] *History of the United States of America: A Guide to Information Sources,* by Ernest Cassara (Detroit: Gale Research Company, 1977). See also the annual *Bibliographic Guide to North American History* [54], which lists new works cataloged by the Library of Congress and the New York Public Library.

There are some American history items in [119] *The American Historical Association's Guide to Historical Literature,* edited by George Frederick Howe and others (New York: Macmillan Company, 1961). The section on the United States, pp. 711–44, was edited by Michael Kraus. This work, now more than thirty years old, will soon be replaced by a new *Guide* to be published in two volumes by Oxford University Press in 1995. John Higham, the first general editor of the project, has been succeeded by Mary Beth Norton; some 350 historians from around the world will contribute to the work, which aims to reflect the great expansion of historical research in recent decades and to make authoritative references in many fields and subfields more generally known among historians.

For researchers interested in public policy and public affairs, a valuable index to books, government documents, periodical literature, and other publications is [120] *Public Affairs Information Service Bulletin*

(*PAIS Bulletin*), 1915–. First issued by the H. W. Wilson Company, it is now published by Public Affairs Information Service, New York. There is an annual cumulative volume with author index and also [121] *Cumulated Subject Index to the P.A.I.S. Annual Bulletin, 1915–1974,* 15 vols. (Arlington, Va.: Carrollton Press, 1977–1978). Subject headings used in the *Bulletin* are given in [122] *PAIS Subject Headings,* 2d ed. (New York: Public Affairs Information Service, 1990). Beginning with January 1991, the *PAIS Bulletin* has been merged with the Public Affairs Information Service's *Foreign Language Index* under the new title [123] *PAIS International in Print,* issued monthly, with quarterly and annual cumulations. This is available online and on CD-ROM.

Bibliographies of Bibliographies

It is often helpful to locate specialized bibliographies devoted to the exact topic, period, or sort of material one has in view, and bibliographies of subject bibliographies are available. The best place to start is [124] *Bibliographies in American History: Guide to Materials for Research,* by Henry Putney Beers, rev. ed. (New York: H. W. Wilson Company, 1942). A sequel to this standard work is [125] *Bibliographies in American History, 1942–1978: Guide to Materials for Research,* by Henry Putney Beers, 2 vols. (Woodbridge, Conn.: Research Publications, 1982), which continues rather than supersedes the original work. Beers's volumes list general bibliographies, works according to broad subject areas, and items arranged by geographical areas. Bibliographies that are parts of books and those that appear in periodicals are included as well as separately published books. More up-to-date American bibliographies are given in [126] *Bibliographies in History,* vol. 1, *An Index to Bibliographies in History Journals and Dissertations Covering the U.S. and Canada* (Santa Barbara, Calif.: ABC-Clio, 1988), material taken from the *America: History and Life* [112] database.

An extensive work with international coverage, including a great many bibliographies pertaining to American history, is [127] *A World Bibliography of Bibliographies and of Bibliographical Catalogues, Calendars, Abstracts, Digests, Indexes, and the Like,* by Theodore Besterman, 4th ed., 5 vols. (Lausanne: Societas Bibliographica, 1965–1966). The first four volumes, with 6,664 columns of entries, contain the list of bibliographies arranged primarily by subject (with geographical divisions under the subject headings where applicable); the fifth volume is a detailed index. This work is limited to separately published bibliographies. It is supplemented by [128] *A World Bibliography of Bibliographies, 1964–1974: A List of Works Represented by Library of Congress Printed Catalog Cards: A Decennial Supplement to Theodore Besterman, A World Bibliography of Bibliographies,* by Alice F. Toomey, 2 vols. (Totowa, N.J.: Rowman and Littlefield, 1977). These two volumes are arranged alphabetically by subjects, which include such entries as United States, Confederate States, New England, Northwest, Southern States, Southwest, West, and also individual states.

An ongoing publication is [129] *Bibliographic Index: A Cumulative Bibliography of Bibliographies* (New York: H. W. Wilson Company, 1945–). Volumes 1–8 are a series of cumulations, each covering a number of years, from 1937 to 1969. From 1969 annual cumulations have been issued; there are paperback issues in April and August as well as the December annual. The *Bibliographic Index* provides a "subject list of bibliographies published separately or appearing as parts of books, pamphlets, and periodicals." Only bibliographies having fifty or more citations are included. This index is also available online.

A new reference work is [130] *Serial Bibliographies and Abstracts in History: An Annotated Guide,* by David Henige (Westport, Conn.: Greenwood Press, 1986). It is international in scope, with 874 entries. See also [131] *Checklist of Bibliographies Appearing in the Bulletin of Bibliography, 1897–1987,* by Naomi Caldwell-Wood and Patrick W. Wood (Westport, Conn.: Meckler, 1989).

An older book, with limited entries but still of some use, is [132] *Historical Bibliographies: A Systematic and Annotated Guide,* by Edith M. Coulter and Melanie Gerstenfeld (Berkeley: University of California Press, 1935), which includes a section on the United States, pp. 130–57. For bibliographies dealing with Americana up to 1800, see [133] "Americana: Selected Bibliographies and Monographs," in *Incunabula and Americana, 1450–1800: A Key to Bibliographical Study,* by Margaret Bingham Stillwell (New York: Columbia University Press, 1931), pp. 341–440.

Specialized Bibliographies

An important guide to materials that are easy to overlook is [134] *Essay and General Literature Index* (New York: H. W. Wilson Company,

1900–). It indexes, by author and subject, articles or essays published in printed books (and thus missed by periodical indexes). Emphasis is on works in the humanities and social sciences. It appears semiannually, with a paper issue in June and an annual cumulation. A permanent cumulation is now published every five years, but initially the cumulations covered longer periods. See also *Essay and General Literature Index: Works Indexed 1900–1969*, which lists all the books analyzed in the 70-year period and the cumulations in which they appear.

Some bibliographies deal with particular topics, localities, or kinds of publications, and there are foreign bibliographies that contain American materials. The following are examples:

[135] *A Comprehensive Bibliography for the Study of American Minorities*, by Wayne Charles Miller and others, 2 vols. (New York: New York University Press, 1976). These volumes provide a classified, annotated bibliography of 29,300 items.

[136] *A Critical Bibliography of Religion in America*, by Nelson R. Burr, 2 parts, vol. 4 of *Religion in American Life*, by James Ward Smith and A. Leland Jameson (Princeton: Princeton University Press, 1961).

[137] *Ethnographic Bibliography of North America*, by George Peter Murdock and Timothy J. O'Leary, 4th ed., 5 vols. (New Haven: Human Relations Area Files Press, 1975). A supplement covering 1973–1987, by M. Marlene Martin and Timothy J. O'Leary, was published in 3 volumes in 1990.

[138] *Guide to American Foreign Relations since 1700*, by Richard Dean Burns (Santa Barbara, Calif.: ABC-Clio, 1983). Sponsored by the Society for Historians of American Foreign Relations (SHAFR). It gives complete citations for 9,000 monographs, journal articles, documents, and other works, plus references to many more.

[139] *Guide to the Study of United States History outside the U.S., 1845–1980*, Lewis Hanke, general editor, 5 vols. (White Plains, N.Y.: Kraus International Publications, 1985). Sponsored by the American Historical Association and the University of Massachusetts, Amherst.

[140] *Pamphlets in American History: A Bibliographic Guide to the Microform Collections*, 4 vols. (Sanford, N.C.: Microfilming Corporation of America, 1979–1983). There originally were four groups of microfiche: Group I contains pamphlets dealing with General Biography, Indians, Revolutionary War, Revolutionary War Biography,

and Women. Group II deals with Civil Liberties, Labor, and Tariffs and Free Trade. Group III deals with Cooperative Societies, Finance, the Mexican War, Socialism, and the War of 1812. Group IV deals with Catholicism and Anti-Catholicism and with the Spanish-American War. The guides have author, title, and subject indexes. A Group V has been added, dealing with the Civil War, the European War, and Mormon Religion, and the series has been taken over by UMI Research Collections, Ann Arbor, Michigan.

[141] *Public Works History in the United States: A Guide to the Literature,* by Suellen M. Hoy and Michael C. Robinson (Nashville: American Association for State and Local History, 1982). Sponsored by the Public Works Historical Society.

[142] *United States History and Historiography in Postwar Soviet Writings, 1945–1970,* by Leo Okinshevich (Santa Barbara, Calif.: ABC-Clio Press, 1976). Titles are given in transliteration, with an English translation supplied.

The [143] *International Bibliography of Historical Sciences,* begun in 1926, is a current ongoing bibliography with annual cumulations that covers material from prehistory to the present. It is a classified list with an author–proper name index. There are a good many United States items.

Subject bibliographies abound, and by using the general bibliographic guides and reference works listed above researchers can make up bibliographies (and bibliographies of bibliographies) on topics in which they are interested. Part Two of the first edition of this *Handbook* [113] provides extensive lists of significant and relatively recent bibliographies and other reference works broken down into special topics: political history, foreign affairs, military history, social history, ethnic groups, women, African Americans, American Indians, education, religion, economic history, science/technology/medicine, regional studies, travel accounts, and chronological periods.

Guides to Related Disciplines

Because historians, from time to time, need to draw on writings in fields related to history, guides to research in those fields may be of use.

[144] *American Studies: An Annotated Bibliography,* by Jack Salzman, 3 vols. (New York: Cambridge University Press, 1986). A one-vol-

ume supplement covering works published 1984–1988 was published in 1990.

[145] *The Information Sources of Political Science,* by Frederick L. Holler, 4th ed. (Santa Barbara, Calif.: ABC-Clio, 1986).

[146] *Political Science: A Guide to Reference and Information Sources,* by Henry E. York (Englewood, Colo.: Libraries Unlimited, 1990).

[147] *The Social Sciences: A Cross-Disciplinary Guide to Selected Sources,* by Nancy L. Herron (Englewood, Colo.: Libraries Unlimited, 1989).

[148] *Sociology: A Guide to Reference and Information Sources,* by Stephen H. Aby (Littleton, Colo.: Libraries Unlimited, 1987).

[149] *Sources of Information in the Social Sciences: A Guide to the Literature,* by William H. Webb and others, 3d ed. (Chicago: American Library Association, 1986).

Guides to Microforms

Since much material of use to American historians is available in microform, it is wise to be aware of reference guides to that material. The following will be of help:

[150] *Guide to Microforms in Print: Author, Title,* and [151] *Guide to Microforms in Print: Subject,* published annually since 1978 by Meckler. They replace earlier publications that began in 1961.

[152] *National Register of Microform Masters,* 1965–1975, 6 vols. (Washington: Library of Congress, 1976), with annual volumes, 1976–1983. New material can be found in *National Union Catalog: Books* [33] and in *Bibliographic Guide to Microform Publications* [53].

[153] *Microform Research Collections: A Guide,* by Suzanne Cates Dodson, 2d ed. (Westport, Conn.: Meckler Publishing, 1984).

[154] *An Index to Microform Collections,* by Ann Niles (Westport, Conn.: Meckler Publishing, 1984).

[155] *Guide to Photocopied Historical Materials in the United States and Canada,* by Richard W. Hale, Jr. (Ithaca, N.Y.: Cornell University Press for the American Historical Association, 1961).

History Journals

Current materials of several types can be located in historical journals. The *Journal of American History,* for example, in its book reviews provides a reasonably comprehensive coverage of new books and in its section on ''Recent Scholarship'' lists periodical articles and dissertations under subject headings. Other general history periodicals can be used for the same purpose; some specialized journals list articles in their specialties.

5

Catalogs of Books and Imprints

Some bibliographers have been concerned with making checklists of all printed works of a given period, region, or subject. Their aim is to produce exhaustive compilations with detailed bibliographical descriptions of each work and its various editions—in some cases looking for variations not only in the editions as a whole but even in the signatures (parts) of a bound volume. This sort of precision and completeness appeals especially to persons who seek variations in literary works that might have meaning for critics, to those concerned with early works and fugitive or elusive publications, and to those interested in the history and development of printing. The interest in printing and printers has led to the use of the word *imprint,* which originally referred to the printer's identification or colophon but which now is used frequently in a broader sense to mean any printed work, whether book, pamphlet, or broadside.

For historians these book catalogs and checklists often have value. They furnish information on what was published in a given period or in a region or by an individual author, and they help to nail down particular works.

National and General Catalogs

An extensive well-known catalog is [156] *Bibliotheca Americana: A Dictionary of Books Relating to America, from Its Discovery to the Present Time,* by Joseph Sabin, continued by Wilberforce Eames and completed by R. W. G. Vail, 29 vols. (New York: Joseph Sabin, 1868–1892; New York: Bibliographical Society of America, 1928–1936). This massive work includes 106,413 numbered items, plus added editions and works mentioned in the notes. The arrangement is by author, with full bibliographical information supplied for each work and in many cases the names of libraries holding copies. There are no title or subject indexes in the original work, but this lack is partially supplied by [157] *Author-Title Index to Joseph Sabin's Dictionary of Books Relating to America,* by John Edgar Molnar, 3 vols. (Metuchen, N.J.: Scarecrow Press, 1974).

The early parts of Sabin will be superseded by [158] *European Americana: A Chronological Guide to Works Printed in Europe Relating to the Americas, 1493–1776.* Prepared as a project of the John Carter Brown Library at Brown University, this catalog lists works chronologically and includes indexes by author, title, and subject. Volume 1 (1493–1600) and volume 2 (1601–1650), edited by John Alden and Dennis C. Landis, were published in 1980 and 1982 by Readex Books; volume 5 (1701–1725) and volume 6 (1726–1750), edited by Dennis Channing Landis, were published by Readex Books in 1987 and 1988. Volumes 3 and 4 (1651–1700) are in progress. These volumes include many titles not included in Sabin.

A work of special interest to American historians is [159] *American Bibliography: A Chronological Dictionary of All Books, Pamphlets and Periodical Publications Printed in the United States of America from the Genesis of Printing in 1639 Down to and Including the Year 1820 (1800), with Bibliographical and Biographical Notes,* by Charles Evans, 12 vols. (Chicago: The author, 1903–1934). This ambitious work includes items arranged by year of publication, provides extensive bibliographical detail, and, wherever possible, notes the location of copies in American libraries. Each volume has indexes to authors, classified subjects, and printers and publishers. Evans intended originally to list publications up to 1820, but eventually he himself carried the catalog only through the letter M of 1799.

This original work, often referred to simply as "Evans," has spawned a number of subsequent publications, which extend or augment Evans's own coverage. Volume 13, compiled by Clifford K. Shipton (Worcester, Mass.: American Antiquarian Society, 1955), starts with the letter N of 1799 and continues through 1800. Volume 14, *Index,* by Roger Pattrell Bristol (Worcester, Mass.: American Antiquarian Society, 1959) is a cumulated author-title index for the whole work. There is also [160] *Index of Printers, Publishers, and Booksellers Indicated by Charles Evans in His American Bibliography,* by Roger Pattrell Bristol (Charlottesville: Bibliographical Society of the University of Virginia, 1961); and [161] *Supplement to Charles Evans' American Bibliography,* by Roger P. Bristol (Charlottesville: University Press of Virginia, for the Bibliographical Society of America and the Bibliographical Society of the University of Virginia, 1970), which adds about 11,200 entries to the Evans listings. An index to the latter work was published in 1971.

The value of the Evans checklist was greatly enhanced by the microprint publication [162] *Early American Imprints, 1639–1800* (New York:

Readex Microprint Corporation). The microprint offers the complete text of all the items listed in Evans's *American Bibliography,* plus 10,035 items that have turned up later (nearly all the items in Bristol's *Supplement*). A guide to this collection, which can serve also as a substitute for the original volumes, is [163] *National Index of American Imprints through 1800: The Short-Title Evans,* by Clifford K. Shipton and James E. Mooney, 2 vols. (Worcester, Mass.: American Antiquarian Society and Barre Publishers, 1969). This index corrects errors in Evans and shows the location of the copy of each item used in the microprint edition. A student with the Readex Microprint edition (or the more recent Readex microfiche) and the short-title index at hand has a magnificent resource for research in early American history. A tape of the *Early American Imprints* entries has been made available, and some libraries that have the text of the items in microform have loaded the tape into their own computerized library catalogs, greatly facilitating use of the collection. These records are also available through RLIN. A North American Imprints Program (NAIP) at the American Antiquarian Society aims ultimately to create a highly detailed, machine-readable catalog of books, pamphlets, and broadsides printed before 1877 in the United States and Canada.

A number of bibliographers have worked to carry forward chronologically the work initiated by Charles Evans. The first of the publications, with regard to period covered, is [164] *American Bibliography: A Preliminary Checklist, 1801–1819,* by Ralph Robert Shaw and Richard H. Shoemaker, 19 vols. (New York: Scarecrow Press, 1953–1963). Arrangement is by author; there is a volume for each year. The initial volumes have been augmented by three volumes: *Addenda, List of Sources, Library Symbols* (1965); *Title Index* (1965); and *Corrections, Author Index* (1966). A further supplementary volume is [165] *American Bibliography: A Preliminary Checklist 1801 to 1819, Printers, Publishers, and Booksellers Index, Geographical Index,* by Frances P. Newton (Metuchen, N.J.: Scarecrow Press, 1983).

A useful addition to the Evans and Shaw/Shoemaker bibliographies is [166] *Maps Contained in the Publications of the American Bibliography, 1639–1819: An Index and Checklist,* by Jim Walsh (Metuchen, N.J.: Scarecrow Press, 1988).

The Shaw and Shoemaker volumes are continued by [167] *A Checklist of American Imprints, 1820–1829,* by Richard H. Shoemaker, 10 vols. (New York: Scarecrow Press, 1964–1971). There is a *Title Index* to these volumes by M. Frances Cooper (Metuchen, N.J.: Scarecrow Press, 1972), and an *Author Index,* by M. Frances Cooper (Metuchen, N.J.: Scarecrow Press, 1973). Additional volumes, beginning with 1830 and expected to run through 1875, have been completed through 1842, edited variously by Gayle Cooper, Scott Bruntjen, and Carol Rinderknecht and published 1972–1992. For the 59,415 bibliographic items described for the period 1830 through 1839 there are two indexes: [168] *A Checklist of American Imprints, 1830–1839: Title Index,* by Carol Rinderknecht, 2 vols. (Metuchen, N.J.: Scarecrow Press, 1989), and [169] *A Checklist of American Imprints, 1830–1839: Author Index,* by Carol Rinderknecht (Metuchen, N.J.: Scarecrow Press, 1989).

The Shoemaker *Checklist* and its continuations have moved deeply into the period covered by an earlier catalog, [170] *Bibliotheca Americana: Catalogue of American Publications, Including Reprints and Original Works, from 1820 to 1852 Inclusive,* by O. A. Roorbach (New York: Orville A. Roorbach, 1852), which has three supplements carrying the catalog to January 1861. These four volumes were continued by [171] *The American Catalogue of Books (Original and Reprints), Published in the United States,* by James Kelly, 2 vols. (New York: J. Wiley and Sons, 1866–1871). The first volume covers the period January 1861 to January 1866; the second extends the coverage to January 1871. Both Roorbach's and Kelly's works are incomplete and sometimes inaccurate, but they are the most general lists for the period after Shoemaker's *Checklist* with its current extensions.

An idiosyncratic catalog of items from Sabin and of other items is [172] *The New Sabin: Books Described by Joseph Sabin and His Successors, Now Described Again on the Basis of Examination of Originals, and Fully Indexed by Title, Subject, Joint Authors, and Institutions and Agencies,* by Lawrence S. Thompson, 10 vols. to date (Troy, N.Y.: Whitston Publishing Company, 1974–). There are topical volumes and sections—on slavery, Lincoln, or Kentucky, for example—and emphasis is placed on items that are available in microform collections, notably those issued by the Lost Cause Press. There is a cumulative index, published in 1986, to volumes 1–10 (entries 1–25,946) of this continuing series.

For books published from the 1870s on there are a number of catalogs with appropriate cumulations that are generally accurate and complete. Although most researchers in United States history may not need to consult them frequently, their existence should be noted. The [173]

American Catalogue (New York: Publishers Weekly, 1880–1911) is the standard list for the period 1876–1910. It was begun by Frederick Leypoldt as a trade bibliography of books in print. The initial work of two volumes has author and title entries of books in print on July 1, 1876, and subject entries; it was supplemented by volumes covering subsequent periods (of 3, 5, or 8 years), with author-title-subject volumes. The [174] *United States Catalog: Books in Print, January 1, 1928*, 4th ed. (New York: H. W. Wilson Company, 1928) succeeded earlier editions, which listed books in print as of 1899, 1902, and 1912. Supplements, entitled *Cumulative Book Index*, have been published for the intervening years, as cumulations or as annual volumes. After the 4th edition of the *United States Catalog* in 1928, the lists are continued by [175] *Cumulative Book Index: A World List of Books in the English Language* (*CBI*) (New York: H. W. Wilson Company, 1933–). A number of cumulations have been issued covering 2–4 years; since 1969 the work has been published annually, since 1987 in two volumes. The cumulations are dictionary catalogs with author, title, and subject entries.

A standard book-trade journal, which lists new publications and books announced for publication is [176] *Publishers Weekly* (New York: R. R. Bowker Company, 1872–), with variations in subtitle and publisher. As a weekly publication reaching back to 1872, it has provided current information on books published in the United States. The [177] *American Book Publishing Record* (*BPR*, later *ABPR*) (New York: R. R. Bowker Company, 1960–) is a monthly publication arranged by subject according to Dewey decimal numbers and indexed by author and title. There are annual cumulations and three sets of five-year cumulations (1960–1974). For longer cumulations see [178] *American Book Publishing Record Cumulative, 1876–1949: An American National Bibliography,* 15 vols. (New York: R. R. Bowker Company, 1980); and [179] *American Book Publishing Record Cumulative, 1950–1977: An American National Bibliography,* 15 vols. (New York: R. R. Bowker Company, 1978). Each of these series has ten volumes devoted to Dewey decimal classifications and separate volumes for fiction, non-Dewey titles, author index, title index, and subject guide. These cumulations were compiled from Library of Congress printed cards and National Union Catalog entries and contain thousands of entries not found in the original volumes of *BPR*. There are about 625,000 entries in the 1876–1949 volumes and about 900,000 entries in the 1950–1977 volumes.

Another collection of information on American books is [180] *Pub-*

lishers Trade List Annual (*PTLA*), which consists of publishers' catalogs bound together alphabetically in one or more large volumes each year. The most recent issue is *Publishers Trade List Annual,* 1991 (New Providence, N.J.: R. R. Bowker, 1991).

The *PTLA* was originally the basis of the data cumulated since 1948 in [181] *Books in Print* (New York: R. R. Bowker Company, 1948–), which since the 1970s has been produced from an expanded database. *Books in Print* now has separate volumes (or sets of volumes) for authors, titles, out-of-print books, and publishers. Beginning in 1957, *Books in Print* has been complemented by [182] *Subject Guide to Books in Print* (New York: R. R. Bowker Company, 1957–), which now includes a *Thesaurus* volume that provides subject headings for searching. Because so many books—including many reprints of old but important works—are published in paperback editions, a researcher may want to use [183] *Paperbound Books in Print* (New York: R. R. Bowker Company, 1955–). It is now issued in two cumulative hardbound volumes each year and has title, author, and subject indexes. There is also a [184] *Books in Print Supplement,* a midyear updating service. R. R. Bowker also publishes six times a year [185] *Forthcoming Books,* which gives information on recently published books and books still to appear. The various *Books in Print* publications are also available online and on CD-ROM.

For books that appear as part of titled series, see [186] *Books in Series: Original, Reprinted, In-Print, and Out-of-Print Books, Published or Distributed in the U.S. in Popular, Scholarly, and Professional Series,* 4th ed., 6 vols. (New York: R. R. Bowker Company, 1985). A supplementary set of three volumes, [187] *Books in Series, 1876–1949* (New York: R. R. Bowker Company, 1982), includes pre-1950 items that do not appear in the 4th edition.

Regional and Subject Catalogs

The general catalogs already cited are reasonably complete for works published in the chief publishing centers, but for locally published material it is wise to use also the checklists that have been produced in large numbers for regional, state, or local areas and in some cases for particular periods of United States history. An old but still useful guide is [188] "Locating the Printed Source Materials for United States History, with a Bibliography of Lists of Regional Imprints," by Douglas C. McMurtrie,

Mississippi Valley Historical Review 31 (December 1944): 369–406. A comprehensive and more recent (although now outdated) listing of bibliographies of regional imprints is in [189] *Guide to the Study of United States Imprints,* by G. Thomas Tanselle, 2 vols. (Cambridge: Harvard University Press, 1971), pp. 5–67. The list is arranged by sections of the United States and by states (with cities and other localities listed alphabetically under the state). Significant new bibliographies of state or regional imprints can be located in the volumes of *American Reference Books Annual* [10].

A special group of checklists of regional imprints was produced in the late 1930s and early 1940s by the Historical Records Survey of the United States Work Projects Administration. A listing of the items in the inventory is included in [190] *Bibliography of Research Projects Reports: Check-List of Historical Records Survey Publications,* by Sargent B. Child and Dorothy P. Holmes (Washington: Federal Works Agency, Work Projects Administration, 1943), and in *Guide to Reference Books* [8]. They are included, as well, in Tanselle's *Guide* [189].

Tanselle's *Guide* is also a good place to begin a search for checklists of imprints by subject. It provides a comprehensive listing under more than 90 headings of what it calls "genre lists"—including, for example, almanacs, biographies, Catholic Americana, etiquette books, frontier literature, Indian captivity narratives, military books, Quaker Americana, sermons, and travel literature. It has a long section, too, of author lists.

6

Book Review Indexes

Extensive research in secondary sources may well entail consideration of critical scholarly reviews of books used. To facilitate that search there are a number of reference works.

History Indexes

The citation of book reviews that is best on target for historians interested in United States history is found in *America: History and Life* [112], for the reviews come in large part from scholarly history journals and provide critical evaluations of the books. For many years there were two issues annually (Part B) devoted specifically to book reviews, which were also cited in the annual indexes. Since 1989 the reviews have been entered under subject headings along with abstracts of articles from periodicals and dissertations; the annual index, of course, provides a cumulated index to them.

Other specialized book review indexes, also, are of value to historians, even though they are not currently published. Such indexes are [191] *An Index to Book Reviews in the Humanities,* 1960–1990 (Williamston, Mich.: Phillip Thomson, 1978–1990), and [192] *Book Review Index to Social Science Periodicals,* by Arnold M. Rzepecki, 4 vols. (Ann Arbor, Mich.: Pierian Press, 1978–1981). Volume 1 of the latter covers 1964–1970, and volumes 2–4 carry coverage to March 1974, when *Social Sciences Index* began. An [193] *Index to Book Reviews in Historical Periodicals,* by John W. Brewster and Joseph A. McLeod (Metuchen, N.J.: Scarecrow Press, 1976–1979), was published in annual volumes covering 1972–1977.

Two retrospective indexes to reviews are [194] *Combined Retrospective Index to Book Reviews in Scholarly Journals, 1886–1974,* 15 vols. (Woodbridge, Conn.: Research Publications, 1979–1982), which provides author and title access to more than one million reviews in over 450 scholarly journals in history, political science, and sociology; and [195] *Combined Retrospective Index to Book Reviews in Humanities Journals, 1802–1974*, 10 vols. (Woodbridge, Conn.: Research Publications, 1982–1984), which provides authors and titles for about 500,000 reviews in more than 150 journals.

General Indexes and Digests

General book review services, although not covering many history journals, still may turn up material of value, and they generally cite early reviews of the books. A standard, widely available work is [196] *Book Review Digest, 1905–* (New York: H. W. Wilson Company, 1905–), a monthly with annual cumulations, which provides brief excerpts from selected reviews. Its coverage of scholarly reviews, however, is limited. There are two cumulative indexes: [197] *Book Review Digest: Author/Title Index, 1905–1974*, by Leslie Dunmore-Leiber, 4 vols. (New York: H. W. Wilson Company, 1976), and [198] *Book Review Digest Author/Title Index, 1975–1984*, by Robert E. Klaum (New York: H. W. Wilson Company, 1986). More comprehensive, although without excerpts, is [199] *Current Book Review Citations, 1976–1982* (New York: H. W. Wilson Company, 1976–1983), which cumulates book review citations from all the Wilson periodical indexes.

Another useful index is [200] *Book Review Index* (Detroit: Gale Research Company, 1965–). It appeared monthly at first but in 1977 changed to bimonthly. It has annual cumulations from the beginning of its publication in 1965. For ease in retrospective searching, there is [201] *Book Review Index: A Master Cumulation, 1965–1984*, by Gary C. Tarbert and Barbara Beach, 10 vols. (Detroit: Gale Research Company, 1985), which cites more than 1,650,000 reviews of approximately 740,500 titles, but a good many American history journals are not included.

Citations of pertinent book reviews also appear in the periodical indexes issued by the H. W. Wilson Company, such as *Readers' Guide to Periodical Literature* [216], *Humanities Index* [223], and *Social Sciences Index* [224], which list the reviews in a separate alphabetical listing following the main index. Major sources for book reviews are *Arts and Humanities Citation Index* [233] and *Social Sciences Citation Index* [234], which can be checked easily by looking for the book author's last name in the "Citations" sections of the indexes.

Two special publications are [202] *The New York Times Book Review Index, 1896–1970*, 5 vols. (New York: New York Times and Arno Press, 1973); and [203] *Reviews in American History,* 1973–, which is not an index to reviews but a journal devoted exclusively to review essays on new and important books in United States history.

Most of the continuing indexes to book reviews cited above (including *America: History and Life* and the H. W. Wilson Company's indexes) are available online and on CD-ROM for recent years. In addition, [204] *Books in Print with Book Reviews Plus* is issued on CD-ROM six times a year. It includes the full text of the reviews, but the reviews cited come from libraries' and publishers' reviewing journals. University Publications of America offers subscriptions to [205] *Scholarly Book Reviews on CD-ROM,* which provides full texts of book reviews from more than 100 scholarly journals, including a segment on history.

7

Guides to Periodical Literature

Many of the general bibliographies and the general history bibliographies provide listings of articles on United States history in periodicals. Of these, *Writings on American History* [105] is perhaps the most important. It included articles (as well as books and other materials) from its beginning in 1902, and from 1973 to its end in 1990 it listed *only* articles. Similarly, *America: History and Life* [111], which began in 1965 as a periodical abstracts publication, continues an extensive coverage of American history articles. Another general American history guide that lists journal articles is the *Harvard Guide to American History* [114]. For retrospective citations, these and other bibliographies and indexes discussed in chapter 2 should be checked early in a research project.

Bibliographies of History Articles

There are some bibliographical guides that pertain particularly to historical periodical literature. One of these is [206] *Recently Published Articles,* which continued the listings of articles by fields that were originally published regularly in the *American Historical Review.* It had spring, summer, and autumn issues each year and appeared from 1976 through 1990 as a separate publication of the American Historical Association. There is a sizable United States section.

The *Journal of American History* [18], in the "Recent Scholarship" section of each issue, lists current periodical literature in American history by subfields; and other, more particular, history journals, such as the [207] *Western Historical Quarterly,* the [208] *Journal of Southern History,* [209] *Labor History,* and a number of state historical journals also provide lists of articles—some appearing in each quarterly issue, others annually or semiannually. Henige's *Serial Bibliographies and Abstracts in History* [130] provides a catalog of such journals as well as of separately published works that appear serially.

An ambitious project to provide a retrospective index to articles in historical journals, which began first as an online database and then appeared as a complete printout of the database, is the [210] *Combined Retrospective Index Set to Journals in History, 1838–1974*, 11 vols. (Washington: Carrollton Press, 1977–1978). It lists 150,000 articles from 234 history journals in English. Nine volumes are arranged by fields, with subject categories and keyword indexes within them; two volumes provide an author index. The citations, however, are severely abbreviated.

General Periodical Indexes

The standard general periodical indexes are frequently of use to historians, even though they are not heavily concerned with scholarly historical articles. The oldest is [211] *An Index to Periodical Literature,* by William Frederick Poole, 3d ed. brought down to January 1882 with the assistance of William I. Fletcher (Boston: James R. Osgood and Company, 1882). Five supplements, with the title *Poole's Index to Periodical Literature,* carry the index through 1906. The index is by subject only and does not contain dates. For authors, use [212] *Cumulative Author Index for Poole's Index to Periodical Literature, 1802–1906,* by C. Edward Wall (Ann Arbor: Pierian Press, 1971). For dates, use [213] *Poole's Index, Date and Volume Key,* by Marion V. Bell and Jean C. Bacon (Chicago: Association of College and Reference Libraries, 1957). Because there are numerous citations of articles in *The Nation,* it is helpful to look at [214] *The Nation: Indexes of Titles and Contributors,* vols. 1–105, 1865–1917, by Daniel C. Haskell, 2 vols. (New York: New York Public Library, 1951–1953).

The 1890s are covered in [215] *The Nineteenth Century Readers' Guide to Periodical Literature,* by Helen Grant Cushing and Adah V. Morris, 2 vols. (New York: H. W. Wilson Company, 1944). This guide provides an author and subject index to 56 periodicals.

Next follows the popular and widely used [216] *Readers' Guide to Periodical Literature* (New York: H. W. Wilson Company, 1905–), which began coverage in 1900 with a small number of popular magazines but has steadily widened its coverage. The *Readers' Guide* gives full information—author, title, magazine, and publication data—but since the periodicals indexed are for the most part general or popular magazines, articles from scholarly historical journals do not appear in great number.

In 1988 Wilson began [217] *Readers' Guide Abstracts,* which in its printed form offers abstracts of about 40 percent of the articles indexed by the *Readers' Guide*; a microfiche version, with coverage from 1984, indexes all the articles except book reviews. The *Readers' Guide* and *Abstracts* are available online and on CD-ROM.

Some of the omissions in the *Readers' Guide* are supplied in [218] *Annual Magazine Subject Index,* 43 vols. (Boston: F. W. Faxon Company, 1908–1952). These annual volumes, issued for the period 1907–1949, provide an index by subject for articles in 356 American, Canadian, and English magazines. The emphasis is on journals not covered by other indexes, and the *Index* includes a great many local and state historical journals of the United States. Because the *Writings on American History* [105] was not published between 1940 and 1947, this *Index* helps to fill in that gap. There is a convenient [219] *Cumulated Magazine Subject Index, 1907–1949,* 2 vols. (Boston: G. K. Hall and Company, 1964), which was formed by cutting apart copies of the annual volumes and pasting the 253,000 individual items together again in a single cumulated list.

Of particular help to historians is the [220] *Social Sciences and Humanities Index* (New York: H. W. Wilson Company), which covered American and English periodicals of a more scholarly nature than those indexed by *Readers' Guide*. It began as [221] *Readers' Guide Supplement,* 2 vols. (1907–1919); from 1920 to 1965 it was called [222] *International Index to Periodicals.* Then in 1974 it was divided into two separate indexes: [223] *Humanities Index* (New York: H. W. Wilson Company, 1974–) and [224] *Social Sciences Index* (New York: H. W. Wilson Company, 1974–).

Some researchers find it useful to keep up to date on current articles by checking the tables of contents of pertinent periodicals. That is now easily done through [225] *Current Contents,* issued by the Institute for Scientific Information in seven editions, of which those for Social and Behavioral Sciences and for Arts and Humanities will interest historians. The former appears weekly, the latter biweekly. They reprint the tables of contents of a large number of journals, including in some cases book reviews. A similar approach to current periodical bibliography is possible through the Internet, connecting to the [226] *UnCover* database of the Colorado Alliance of Research Libraries (CARL). Beginning in 1988, the database contains articles from over 12,000 journals received by CARL member libraries, which can be searched by tables of contents.

University Microfilms International has issued on microfilm the [227] *American Periodicals Series, 1741–1900,* which offers the full text of American periodicals from the 18th and 19th centuries. There are three parts: *American Periodicals, 18th Century (APS I)*; *American Periodicals, 1800–1850 (APS II)*; and *American Periodicals, 1850–1900, Civil War and Reconstruction (APS III)*. More than 1,100 titles are included on 2,770 reels of microfilm. For a general index to the periodical titles, not to the contents, see [228] *American Periodicals Series, 1741–1900: An Index to the Microfilm Collections,* by Jean Hoornstra and Trudy Heath (Ann Arbor: University Microfilms International, 1979), which includes title, general subject, editor, and reel number indexes. A very valuable supplement is a detailed computer-generated contents index to the periodicals, now in process: [229] *Index to American Periodicals of the 1700s,* keyed to University Microfilms *APS I,* 2 vols. (Indianapolis: Computer Indexed Systems, 1989), and [230] *Index to American Periodicals of the 1800s,* keyed to University Microfilms *APS II,* 11 vols. projected (Indianapolis: Computer Indexed Systems, 1989–). As of 1990 there were 5 volumes for the period 1800–1825.

An older card file index, [231] *Index to Early American Periodical Literature, 1728–1870,* was produced at New York University as a WPA project in the 1930s, indexing about 350 early periodicals. A microprint publication of part of this card file is [232] *Index to Early American Periodicals to 1850,* by Nelson F. Adkins (New York: Readex Microprint Corporation, 1964). The Catalogue Department of Washington Square Library, New York University, in the 1940s issued pamphlets that printed material from the index on Edgar Allen Poe, Walt Whitman, Ralph Waldo Emerson, and French fiction.

Citation Indexes

Two vast bibliographic databases essential for historians are [233] *Arts and Humanities Citation Index* (Philadelphia: Institute for Scientific Information, 1976–) and [234] *Social Sciences Citation Index* (Philadelphia: Institute for Scientific Information, 1979–). Modeled on the *Science Citation Index* (1961–), each of these two indexes is divided into a Citation Index, which provides lists of journal articles in which a particular work is cited; a Permuterm Subject Index, which provides access through keywords in titles of articles; a Source Index, which indicates articles of which citations are made; and a Corporate Index, which indicates material produced by organizations and institutions. The *Arts and Humanities Citation Index* indexes more than 2,000 journals, some comprehensively and some selectively, more than 200 of which are history journals. The *Social Sciences Citation Index* indexes more than 2,600 journals, but fewer than 50 are history journals. There are massive multi-year cumulations for each index. Both indexes are available online and on CD-ROM and are regularly updated.

Starting with a known article on a given subject, the researcher can find articles that cited it, thus accumulating titles of articles that might be on the same or related topics. In turn, these articles can be checked for works that cite them, and so on. The word indexes will also lead to useful articles, and the source indexes are in effect bibliographies. Use of the citation indexes is complicated, but instructions are given in each volume. For wise advice about using them effectively, see Mann's *Guide to Library Research Methods* [16], pp. 53–54, 61–65.

Machine-Readable Periodical Databases

For recent periodical literature, a researcher can be helped by electronic versions of standard printed periodical indexes and by special databases available on CD-ROM. Some of these machine-readable databases are noted in appropriate places throughout the *Handbook,* but it is good to recall that all of the periodical indexes, general and special, published by the H. W. Wilson Company are available both online (WILSONLINE) through various vendors and on CD-ROM (WILSONDISC) for recent years. In addition, for current general periodicals many libraries will provide one of the following on CD-ROM:

[235] *InfoTrac General Periodicals Index,* produced by the Information Access Company in both an academic library and a public library edition. The database indexes more than 1,100 publications and includes some abstracts; in addition it covers 60 days of indexing of the *New York Times, Wall Street Journal,* and *Christian Science Monitor.* The monthly updated discs contain the most current four years of data, and back files are available that provide an additional four years of data. A small minority of the journals indexed are history journals.

[236] *Periodical Abstracts Ondisc: Research II Edition,* one of the *ProQuest* databases provided by University Microfilms International

(UMI), which indexes and abstracts from 1,200 general reference publications, with six months of the *Wall Street Journal* and the *New York Times*. In 1992 it had three discs: two back file discs covering 1986–1988 and 1989–1990 and a current-year disc that presents records from 1991 to the present; these will be updated as time passes. In general, the only American historical journals included are important national and regional ones.

The broad possibilities for searching and for manipulating the data that these databases provide make them especially attractive, and they are useful for checking recent book reviews. But it must be remembered that they index only recent or current materials, much of which may be of little interest to the historical researcher.

Periodical Indexes for Special Topics

A researcher in United States history can often find valuable articles listed in specialized periodical indexes. Some of these are ongoing publications, which usually appear quarterly with annual or biennial cumulations. The following are typical examples:

[237] *Access: The Supplementary Index to Periodicals.* Published since 1975 by John Gordon Burke Publisher, Chicago. Indexes periodicals not indexed by other general periodical indexes. Three issues a year.

[238] *Air University Library Index to Military Periodicals,* 1949–. Published by Air University Library, Maxwell Air Force Base, Alabama. Quarterly with annual cumulations.

[239] *Alternative Press Index: An Index to Alternative and Radical Publications,* 1969–. Baltimore: Alternative Press Center. Quarterly.

[240] *Catholic Periodical Index,* 1930–. Title changed with vol. 14 (1967–1968) to [241] *Catholic Periodical and Literature Index.* Vols. 1–13, New York: H. W. Wilson Company; vol. 14–, Haverford, Penn.: Catholic Library Association. In 1992 (vol. 27) it began publishing quarterly, with annual cumulations. There are four sections: Subject Index, Author and Editor Index, Book Title Index, and Book Review Author Index.

[242] *Current Index to Journals in Education (CIJE),* 1969–. Publisher varies. A project of the Education Resources Information Center (ERIC). It is published monthly and cumulated semiannually. See

also [243] *Current Index to Journals in Education (CIJE): Cumulated Author Index, 1969–1984* (Phoenix: Oryx Press, 1985).

[244] *Education Index,* 1929–. New York: H. W. Wilson Company. Issued monthly with annual cumulations. Chiefly a periodical index, but with some yearbooks and monographs.

[245] *Index to Black Periodicals,* 1988–. Published by G. K. Hall and Company, this publication began with a 10-year cumulation, 1950–1959, and was published under varying titles (*Index to Periodical Articles by and about Negroes* and *Index to Periodical Articles by and about Blacks*).

[246] *Index to Religious Periodical Literature,* 1949–. Published by the American Theological Library Association. Title changed with vol. 13 (1976–1977) to [247] *Religion Index One: Periodicals (RIO).* Biennial cumulations but annual cumulations beginning with vol. 17 (1985).

[248] *Index to U.S. Government Periodicals,* 1970–. Chicago: Infordata International. Issued quarterly with annual cumulations. Online and on CD-ROM.

[249] *Women's Studies Index, 1989.* Published by G. K. Hall and Company in 1992; presumably to be annual.

In addition, see the indexes to legal periodical literature listed in chapter 16. There are also current periodical indexes in such fields as business, economics, literature, and art.

In addition to the ongoing indexes, there are a number of closed series or one-time publications that provide bibliographies of periodical articles on special subjects. Among them are the following:

[250] *The Arizona Index: A Subject Index to Periodical Articles about the State,* by Donald M. Powell and Virginia E. Rice, 2 vols. (Boston: G. K. Hall and Company, 1978).

[251] *Articles in American Studies, 1954–1968: A Cumulation of the Annual Bibliographies from American Quarterly,* by Hennig Cohen, 2 vols. (Ann Arbor, Mich.: Pierian Press, 1972).

[252] *Chicano Periodical Index: A Cumulative Index to Selected Chicano Periodicals between 1967 and 1978* (Boston: G. K. Hall and Company, 1981).

[253] *Index to Economic Journals, 1886–1959,* prepared under the auspices of the American Economic Association, 5 vols. (Homewood, Ill.: Richard D. Irwin, 1961–1962).

[254] *Index to Labor Articles,* 27 vols. (New York: Rand School of Social Sciences, 1926–1953).

[255] *Periodical Literature on the American Revolution: Historical Research and Changing Interpretations, 1895–1970,* by Ronald M.
Gephart (Washington: Library of Congress, 1971).

[256] *Periodical Literature on United States Cities: A Bibliography and
Subject Guide,* by Barbara Smith Shearer and Benjamin F. Shearer
(Westport, Conn.: Greenwood Press, 1983).

It may sometimes be necessary to seek periodical articles in areas
outside American history strictly conceived. Lists of guides to such peri-
odical literature are provided in [257] *Periodical Indexes in the Social
Sciences and Humanities: A Subject Guide,* by Lois A. Harzfeld
(Metuchen, N.J.: Scarecrow Press, 1978), and [258] *Subject Guide to
Periodical Indexes and Review Indexes,* by Jean Spealman Kujoth
(Metuchen, N.J.: Scarecrow Press, 1969).

For a list of periodicals indexed by various indexing services, see
[259] *Indexed Periodicals: A Guide to 170 Years of Coverage in 33 Indexing Services,* by Joseph V. Marconi (Ann Arbor, Mich.: Pierian Press,
1976), and [260] *The Index and Abstract Directory: An International
Guide to Services and Serials Coverage* (Birmingham, Ala.: EBSCO
Publishing, 1989). Note also that *Ulrich's International Periodicals Directory* [287] and *New Serial Titles* [262] indicate abstracting and indexing services that cover a given periodical.

Union Lists

Once a bibliography of articles pertinent to one's research is accumulated, the problem arises of finding the issues of the journals in which the
articles appear, if they are not available in local libraries. The answer lies
in union lists of periodicals, which contain bibliographical data on the
publications and supply information about the location of the issues—
that is, which libraries hold the title and which issues each library has on
file. The indispensable general guide is [261] *Union List of Serials in Libraries in the United States and Canada,* 3d ed., by Edna Brown Titus, 5
vols. (New York: H. W. Wilson Company, 1965), which supersedes earlier editions by Winifred Gregory and their supplements. It lists more
than 156,000 journals issued before 1950 and the holdings of 956 libraries. This *Union List of Serials* is supplemented by [262] *New Serial*

Titles, 1950–1970: A Union List of Serials Commencing after December 31, 1949, 4 vols. (Washington: Library of Congress; New York: R. R. Bowker Company, 1973). There are also monthly and annual issues of *New Serial Titles,* with multiyear cumulations. Beginning in 1981, *New Serial Titles* became a product of a computerized cooperative program now called the CONSER (Cooperative Online Serials) Program. It also indicates those titles that are indexed or abstracted by indexing and abstracting services.

For access by subject, see [263] *Subject Index to New Serial Titles, 1950–1965* (Ann Arbor, Mich.: Pierian Press, 1968); and [264] *New Serial Titles, 1950–1970, Subject Guide,* 2 vols. (New York: R. R. Bowker Company, 1975).

The *Union List of Serials* is only one—although the most important—of a large number of union lists of periodicals and newspapers. For a guide to such lists, see [265] *Union Lists of Serials: A Bibliography,* by Ruth S. Freitag (Washington: Government Printing Office, 1964). This volume, international in coverage, refers to 1,218 union lists; it is arranged geographically and then alphabetically in each section.

Catalogs and Directories of Periodicals

Information about journals and other serial publications can be found in catalogs or directories of periodicals. For American history periodicals, see [266] *Historical Periodicals Directory,* by Eric H. Boehm, Barbara H. Pope, and Marie S. Ensign, vol. 1, *USA and Canada* (Santa Barbara, Calif.: ABC-Clio, 1981). English-language journals are listed and annotated in [267] *History Journals and Serials: An Analytical Guide,* by Janet Fyfe (Westport, Conn.: Greenwood Press, 1986).

There are also a number of specialized catalogs of periodicals that may be of use for United States history. Some of them are union lists. The following are examples:

[268] *The Afro-American Periodical Press, 1838–1909,* by Penelope L. Bullock (Baton Rouge: Louisiana State University Press, 1981).

[269] *American Labor Union Periodicals: A Guide to Their Location,* by Bernard G. Naas and Carmelita S. Sakr (Ithaca: Cornell University Press, 1956).

[270] *American Women's Magazines: An Annotated Historical Guide,* by Nancy K. Humphreys (New York: Garland Publishing, 1989).

[271] *Bibliography of Genealogy and Local History Periodicals with Union List of Major U.S. Collections,* by Michael Barren Clegg (Fort Wayne, Ind.: Allen County Public Library Foundation, 1990).

[272] *Black Journals of the United States,* by Walter C. Daniel (Westport, Conn.: Greenwood Press, 1982).

[273] *Catholic Serials of the Nineteenth Century in the United States: A Descriptive Bibliography and Union List,* by Eugene Paul Willging and Herta Hatzfeld, 2d ser., 15 parts (Washington: Catholic University of America Press, 1959–1968).

[274] *Ethnic Periodicals in Contemporary America: An Annotated Guide,* by Sandra L. Jones Ireland (Westport, Conn.: Greenwood Press, 1990).

[275] *From Radical Left to Extreme Right: A Bibliography of Current Periodicals of Protest, Controversy, Advocacy, or Dissent,* by Gail Skidmore and Theodore Jurgen Spahn, 3d ed. (Metuchen, N.J.: Scarecrow Press, 1987).

[276] *Guide to Periodicals in Education and Its Academic Disciplines,* by William L. Camp and Bryan L. Schwark, 2d ed. (Metuchen, N.J.: Scarecrow Press, 1975).

[277] *The Immigrant Labor Press in North America, 1840s-1970s: An Annotated Bibliography,* by Dirk Hoerder and Christiane Harzig, 3 vols. (Westport, Conn.: Greenwood Press, 1987).

[278] *Index to Southern Periodicals,* by Sam G. Riley (Westport, Conn.: Greenwood Press, 1986).

[279] *Military Periodicals: United States and Selected International Journals and Newspapers,* by Michael E. Unsworth (Westport, Conn.: Greenwood Press, 1990).

[280] *Native American Periodicals and Newspapers, 1828–1982: Bibliography, Publishing Record, and Holdings,* by James P. Danky and Maureen E. Hady (Westport, Conn.: Greenwood Press, 1984).

[281] *The Oxbridge Directory of Ethnic Periodicals* (New York: Oxbridge Communications, 1979).

[282] *Radical Periodicals in America, 1890–1950,* by Walter Goldwater, rev. ed. (New Haven: Yale University Library, 1966).

[283] *Religious Periodicals Directory,* by Graham Cornish (Santa Barbara, Calif.: ABC-Clio, 1986).

[284] *Religious Periodicals of the United States: Academic and Scholarly Journals,* by Charles H. Lippy (Westport, Conn.: Greenwood Press, 1986).

[285] *Undergrounds: A Union List of Alternative Periodicals in Libraries of the United States and Canada,* by James P. Danky (Madison: State Historical Society of Wisconsin, 1974).

[286] *Women's Periodicals and Newspapers from the 18th Century to 1981: A Union List of the Holdings of Madison, Wisconsin, Libraries,* by James P. Danky, Maureen E. Hady, Barry Christopher Noonan, and Neil E. Strache (Boston: G. K. Hall and Company, 1982).

Finally, historical researchers should be acquainted with general directories of periodicals. Listed here are current editions, which are updated annually.

[287] *Ulrich's International Periodicals Directory, 1992–93,* 31st ed., 3 vols. (New Providence, N.J.: R. R. Bowker, 1992). First published in 1932, this work now contains information on nearly 126,000 serials published throughout the world, under 788 subject headings. It indicates abstracting and indexing services that cover a given serial and includes notations of those available online and on CD-ROM. A supplement, [288] *Ulrich's Update,* appears three times a year.

[289] *Gale Directory of Publications and Broadcast Media: An Annual Guide to Publications and Broadcasting Stations, 1993,* 125th ed., 3 vols. (Detroit: Gale Research, 1993). Formerly called *Ayer Directory of Publications,* which began in 1869, it covers the United States and Canada. The entries are arranged by states and provinces.

[290] *The Standard Periodical Directory, 1992,* 15th ed. (New York: Oxbridge Communications, 1992). Provides data on more than 75,000 periodicals in the United States and Canada, arranged under 251 subject headings. Includes an alphabetical list of all periodicals that are available online.

Histories of American Magazines

Anyone working with American periodical literature will find great help in understanding the nature and importance of individual journals in [291] *A History of American Magazines,* by Frank Luther Mott, 5 vols. (vol. 1, New York: D. Appleton and Company, 1930; vols. 2–5, Cambridge: Harvard University Press. 1938–1968). For the history of some magazines in the early nineteenth century, see [292] *A History and Bibliography of American Magazines, 1810–1820,* by Neal L. Edgar

(Metuchen, N.J.: Scarecrow Press, 1975). See also [293] *The Ethnic Press in the United States: A Historical Analysis and Handbook,* by Sally M. Miller (Westport, Conn.: Greenwood Press, 1987), and [294] *Magazines of the American South,* by Sam G. Riley (Westport, Conn.: Greenwood Press, 1986).

8

Manuscript Guides

A serious research project in United States history usually requires a search for unique manuscript materials. A great many libraries and other repositories have collected historically significant manuscripts and organized them for use. The documents are variously referred to as manuscript collections, special collections (which frequently include other kinds of material besides manuscripts), and archives (although this term most properly refers to the official records of an organization or institution). Some of the more important collections of documents are now available in microform, often with an accompanying printed guide or index. A general introduction to the use of such unpublished material is [295] *Research in Archives: The Use of Unpublished Primary Sources,* by Philip C. Brooks (Chicago: University of Chicago Press, 1969). It describes various kinds of sources and offers advice about using them.

General Guides to Manuscripts

The most comprehensive and important guide to manuscript collections in the United States is the [296] *National Union Catalog of Manuscript Collections (NUCMC)*, prepared by the Library of Congress. It began publication in 1962 and has had a variety of publishers; since 1966 it has been issued by the Library of Congress. Publication has been in volumes covering either single years or multiyear sequences, beginning with volumes for 1959–1961. Each entry gives the name of the collection, its location, years covered, size, donors, and a brief description of contents, including persons, places, and events involved. The collections consist mostly of personal papers—"manuscript or typescript, originals or copies, of letters, memoranda, diaries, accounts, log books, drafts, etc." Beginning in 1970 oral history interview transcripts and collections containing sound recordings are listed. There are separate indexes for groups of years, or such indexes are contained in appropriate volumes of the series. It is necessary to make sure that all the indexes are checked, since *NUCMC* is a continuing series, and the new volumes contain new entries, not cumulations. Indexes provide access by persons, corporate bodies, and subjects. The preface to the 1990 catalog, published in 1992, indicates that "since its beginnings this catalog has published descriptions of approximately 62,455 collections located in 1,364 different repositories and has indexed them by approximately 706,455 references to topical subjects and personal, family, corporate, and geographical names."

There is an [297] *Index to Personal Names in the National Union Catalog of Manuscript Collections, 1959–1984*, 2 vols. (Alexandria, Va.: Chadwyck-Healey, 1988), which brings together in a single alphabetical list the personal and family names (about 200,000 names) that appear in the descriptions of the manuscript collections cataloged from 1959 to 1984. It also contains corrections and revisions.

A smaller, older, but still very useful work is [298] *A Guide to Archives and Manuscripts in the United States*, by Philip M. Hamer (New Haven: Yale University Press, 1961). Sponsored by the National Historical Publications Commission, the volume is not a union catalog but a guide to direct the researcher to the most useful sources. It includes references to 1,300 repositories, noting, among other collections, the personal papers of more than 7,600 individuals. The material is arranged by repository (alphabetically by state and then by city), with a description of the contents, including individual names of persons appearing in the collections. Published guides to individual collections are noted, and there is a detailed index. Since all this is in a single volume, the work is much easier to use than the printed volumes of *NUCMC*, but of course its coverage is more limited.

An interesting guide to elusive manuscripts for the diligent researcher is [299] *American Manuscripts, 1763–1815: An Index to Documents Described in Auction Records and Dealers' Catalogues*, by Helen Cripe and Diane Campbell (Wilmington, Del.: Scholarly Resources, 1977).

The huge manuscript holdings of the National Archives, including the numerous collections of papers of government officials in the presidential libraries, are noted in chapter 14.

Guides to Individual Repositories and Collections

A thorough search for manuscripts will often require attention to particular repositories and the collections that they hold. A guide to such institutions is [300] *Directory of Archives and Manuscript Repositories in the United States,* 2d ed. (Phoenix: Oryx Press, for the National Historical Publications and Records Commission, 1988), which replaces an edition published by the National Historical Publications and Records Commission in 1978. The volume provides information for about 4,225 repositories. The descriptions of the actual collections are minimal, but there are references to Hamer's *Guide,* to *NUCMC,* and to other printed finding aids. Arrangement is by state, then by city and repository. There are indexes of subjects and of repositories.

Of more limited scope are [301] *Directory of College and University Archives in the United States and Canada* (Chicago: Society of American Archivists, 1980), and [302] *Directory of Business Archives in the United States and Canada,* 4th ed. (Chicago: Society of American Archivists, 1990).

Many of the manuscript repositories and, in some cases, specific collections of documents have detailed published guides, which should be checked before use is made of the collections. An extensive listing of guides to material in particular repositories is provided in the *Directory of Archives and Manuscript Repositories* [300]. Printed guides are noted for every repository for which they are available, including general subject guides that refer to material in the collections and specific guides to the collections themselves. A special note is added if there are nonprinted guides available at the repository. The lists in the *Directory* are extensive and give the researcher essential help in searching out and using the sources. Hamer's *Guide to Archives and Manuscripts* [298] also provides titles of guides to the repositories it lists, and it has a convenient "Note on Bibliographical Guides," pp. xix–xx, which indicates major guides to manuscript collections.

An older, pioneer bibliography is [303] "Guides to American History Manuscript Collections in Libraries of the United States," by Ray Allen Billington, *Mississippi Valley Historical Review* 38 (December 1951): 467–96. It was printed as a pamphlet by Peter Smith, New York, in 1952.

A new publishing venture, [304] *National Inventory of Documentary Sources in the United States* (Teaneck, N.J.: Chadwyck-Healey, 1983–), aims to supply in microfiche (with printed or computer printout indexes) not simply a *list* of printed guides and finding aids, but the complete publications themselves. There are four series: 1. *Federal Records,* including 1,500 finding aids for records in the National Archives,

Smithsonian Institution, and Presidential Libraries; 2. *Manuscript Division, Library of Congress,* with registers of 772 collections in the Manuscript Division; 3. *State Archives, Libraries and Historical Societies,* including finding aids, card catalogs, and indexes (an ongoing, open-ended series); and 4. *Academic Libraries and Other Repositories,* with detailed listings and indexes (an ongoing, open-ended series). The publisher notes: "NUCMC describes the holdings of repositories down to collection level. The National Inventory describes collections down to box, folder or even item level." If researchers have this resource available, they can thoroughly check out a collection before they travel to a repository to use it.

The following is a partial list of guides to specific repositories, illustrating the kinds of works that are available, especially those that have appeared in recent years. The list is arranged alphabetically by repository.

[305] *Manuscript Catalog of the American Jewish Archives,* Cincinnati, 4 vols. (Boston: G. K. Hall and Company, 1971). A supplement was published in 1978 and a second supplement on microfiche in 1991.

[306] *Guide to the Manuscript Collections at the University of Alaska, Anchorage,* by Dennis F. Walle and Carolyn J. Bowers (Fairbanks: University of Alaska Press, 1990).

[307] *Catalogue of the Manuscript Collections of the American Antiquarian Society,* 4 vols. (Boston: G. K. Hall and Company, 1979).

[308] *Catalog of Manuscripts in the American Philosophical Society Library,* 10 vols. (Westport, Conn.: Greenwood Publishing Corporation, 1970).

[309] *A New Guide to the Collections in the Library of the American Philosophical Society,* by J. Stephen Catlett (Philadelphia: American Philosophical Society, 1987). Replaces a *Guide* by Whitfield J. Bell and Murphy D. Smith published in 1966.

[310] *Documents of Southwestern History: A Guide to the Manuscript Collections of the Arizona Historical Society,* by Charles C. Colley (Tucson: Arizona Historical Society, 1972).

[311] *Manuscripts in Baker Library: A Guide to Sources for Business, Economic and Social History,* by Robert W. Lovett and Eleanor G. Bishop, 4th ed. (Boston: Baker Library, Graduate School of Business Administration, Harvard University, 1978).

[312] *Guide to the Manuscript Collections of the Bancroft Library,* by

Dale L. Morgan and George P. Hammond, 2 vols. (Berkeley: University of California Press, 1963–1972).

[313] *Guide to Manuscripts in the Bentley Historical Library,* by Thomas E. Powers and William H. McNitt (Ann Arbor: University of Michigan, 1976). This library houses the Michigan Historical Collections.

[314] *Guide to the Archives of the Archdiocese of Boston,* by James M. O'Toole (New York: Garland Publishing, 1982).

[315] *Guide to Manuscript Collections,* Western History Collections, University of Colorado, 2d ed., by Ellen Arguimbau, Doris Mitterling, and John A. Brennan (Boulder, Colo.: Western History Collections, University of Colorado, 1982).

[316] *Guide to the Cataloged Collections in the Manuscript Department of the William R. Perkins Library, Duke University,* by Richard C. Davis and Linda Angle Miller (Santa Barbara, Calif.: Clio Books, 1980).

[317] *A Guidebook to Manuscripts in the Library of the Thomas Gilcrease Institute of American History and Art,* by Mrs. H. H. Keene (Tulsa: Thomas Gilcrease Institute of American History and Art, 1969).

[318] *Catalogue of Manuscripts in the Houghton Library, Harvard University,* 8 vols. (Alexandria, Va.: Chadwyck-Healey, 1986–1987). Reproduces the library's card file of manuscripts with contents as of April 1985.

[319] *Guide to American Historical Manuscripts in the Huntington Library* (San Marino, Calif.: Huntington Library, 1979).

[320] *Manuscripts Guide to Collections at the University of Illinois at Urbana-Champaign,* by Maynard J. Brichford, Robert M. Sutton, and Dennis F. Walle (Urbana: University of Illinois Press, 1976).

[321] *Guide to the Manuscript Collections of the Indiana Historical Society and Indiana State Library,* by Eric Pumroy and Paul Brockman (Indianapolis: Indiana Historical Society, 1986).

[322] *The Manuscript Collections of the Maryland Historical Society,* by Avril J. M. Pedley (Baltimore: Maryland Historical Society, 1968).

[323] *Catalog of Manuscripts of the Massachusetts Historical Society,* 7 vols. (Boston: G. K. Hall and Company, 1969). A supplement of 2 vols. was published in 1980.

[324] *Guide to the Personal Papers in the Manuscript Collections of the Minnesota Historical Society,* by Grace Lee Nute and Gertrude W. Ackermann (St. Paul: Minnesota Historical Society, 1935). This is

followed by [325] *Manuscript Collections of the Minnesota Historical Society: Guide Number 2*, by Lucile M. Kane and Kathryn A. Johnson (1955), and [326] *Manuscript Collections of the Minnesota Historical Society: Guide Number 3*, by Lydia A. Lucas (1977).

[327] *Catalog of Manuscripts at the National Anthropological Archives*, National Museum of Natural History, Smithsonian Institution, 4 vols. (Boston: G. K. Hall and Company, 1975).

[328] *A Guide to the Manuscript Collections at the Nevada Historical Society*, by L. James Higgins (Reno: Nevada Historical Society, 1975).

[329] *Guide to the Manuscript Collections of the New Jersey Historical Society*, by Don C. Skemer and Robert C. Morris (Newark: New Jersey Historical Society, 1979).

[330] *A Guide to the Manuscript Collections of the New-York Historical Society*, by Arthur J. Breton, 2 vols. (Westport, Conn.: Greenwood Press, 1972).

[331] *Dictionary Catalog*, Manuscript Division, New York Public Library, 2 vols. (Boston: G. K. Hall and Company, 1967).

[332] *Guide to Private Manuscript Collections in the North Carolina State Archives*, 3d rev. ed., by Barbara T. Cain (Raleigh: Division of Archives and History, North Carolina Department of Cultural Resources, 1981).

[333] *The Southern Historical Collection: A Guide to Manuscripts*, University of North Carolina Library, by Susan Sokol Blosser and Clyde Norman Wilson, Jr., (Chapel Hill: University of North Carolina Library, 1970). A *Supplementary Guide to Manuscripts, 1970–1975*, by Everard H. Smith III, was published in 1976.

[334] *Guide to Manuscripts at the Ohio Historical Society*, by Andrea D. Lentz (Columbus: Ohio Historical Society, 1972).

[335] *Guide to the Manuscript Collections of the Presbyterian Church, U.S.*, by Robert Benedetto and Betty K. Walker (Westport, Conn.: Greenwood Press, 1990).

[336] *South Carolina Historical Society Manuscript Guide*, by David Moltke-Hansen and Sallie Doscher (Charleston: South Carolina Historical Society, 1979).

[337] *The University of Texas Archives: A Guide to the Historical Manuscripts Collections in the University of Texas Library*, by Chester V. Kielman (Austin: University of Texas Press, 1967).

[338] *Guide to Archives and Manuscript Collections in Selected Utah Repositories: A Machine-Readable Edition* (Salt Lake City: Utah State Historical Society, 1991). Available in a variety of formats.

[339] *Preliminary Guide to the Manuscript Collection of the U.S. Military Academy Library,* by J. Thomas Russell (West Point, N.Y.: U.S. Military Academy, 1968).

[340] *Guide to Manuscripts and Archives in the West Virginia Collection,* by James W. Hess (Morgantown: West Virginia University Library, 1974).

[341] *A Guide to the Manuscripts and Archives of the Western Reserve Historical Society,* by Kermit J. Pike (Cleveland: Western Reserve Historical Society, 1972).

[342] *Guide to the Manuscripts of the Wisconsin Historical Society,* by Alice E. Smith (Madison: State Historical Society of Wisconsin, 1944). This is continued by *Supplement Number One,* by Josephine L. Harper and Sharon C. Smith (1957), and *Supplement Number Two,* by Josephine L. Harper (1966).

[343] *A Catalogue of Manuscripts in the Collection of Western Americana Founded by William Robertson Coe, Yale University Library,* by Mary C. Withington (New Haven: Yale University Press, 1952).

Guides to Particular Subjects

A number of guides direct the researcher to materials on particular subjects. The following list, arranged alphabetically by title, gives some examples.

[344] *Afro-American Sources in Virginia: A Guide to Manuscripts,* by Michael Plunkett (Charlottesville: University Press of Virginia, 1990).

[345] *American Diaries in Manuscript, 1580–1954: A Descriptive Bibliography,* by William Matthews (Athens: University of Georgia Press, 1974).

[346] *Catalogue of the Frederick W. and Carrie S. Beinecke Collection of Western Americana,* vol. I, *Manuscripts,* by Jeanne M. Goddard, Charles Kritzler, and Archibald Hanna (New Haven: Yale University Press, 1965).

[347] *Civil War Manuscripts: A Guide to Collections in the Manuscript Division of the Library of Congress,* by John R. Sellers (Washington: Library of Congress, 1986).

[348] *Confederate Research Sources: A Guide to Archive Collections,* by James C. Neagles (Salt Lake City: Ancestry Publishing, 1986).

[349] *The French and British in the Old Northwest: A Bibliographical Guide to Archive and Manuscript Sources,* by Henry Putney Beers (Detroit: Wayne State University Press, 1964).

[350] *French and Spanish Records of Louisiana: A Bibliographical Guide to Archive and Manuscript Sources,* by Henry Putney Beers (Baton Rouge: Louisiana State University Press, 1989).

[351] *The French in North America: A Bibliographical Guide to French Archives, Reproductions, and Research Missions,* by Henry Putney Beers (Baton Rouge: Louisiana State University Press, 1957).

[352] *The Fur Trade in Minnesota: An Introductory Guide to Manuscript Sources,* by Bruce M. White (St. Paul: Minnesota Historical Society, 1977).

[353] *Guide to Catholic Indian Mission and School Records in Midwest Repositories,* by Philip C. Bantin and Mark G. Thiel (Milwaukee: Department of Special Collections and University Archives, Marquette University, 1984).

[354] *Guide to Manuscripts Relating to American Indians in the Library of the American Philosophical Society,* by John F. Freeman (Philadelphia: American Philosophical Society, 1966). A supplement by Daythal Kendall was published by the Society in 1982.

[355] *A Guide to Regional Manuscript Collections in the Division of Manuscripts, University of Oklahoma Library,* by A. M. Gibson (Norman: University of Oklahoma Press, 1960).

[356] *A Guide to Shaker Manuscripts in the Library of the Western Reserve Historical Society,* by Kermit J. Pike (Cleveland: Western Reserve Historical Society, 1974).

[357] *Guide to the Heartman Manuscripts on Slavery,* Xavier University, New Orleans (Boston: G. K. Hall and Company, 1982).

[358] *A Guide to the Manuscripts Relating to the History of the British Empire, 1748–1776,* by Lawrence Henry Gipson, vol. 15, *The British Empire before the American Revolution* (New York: Alfred A. Knopf, 1970). A good deal pertains specifically to the American colonies.

[359] *A Guide to the Principal Sources for American Civilization, 1800–1900, in the City of New York: Manuscripts,* by Harry J. Carman and Arthur W. Thompson (New York: Columbia University Press, 1960). Arranged under broad subject categories.

[360] *Lafayette: A Guide to the Letters, Documents, and Manuscripts in the United States,* by Louis Gottschalk, Phyllis S. Pestieau, and Linda J. Pike (Ithaca: Cornell University Press, 1975). A chronological calendar with an indication of the location of each item.

[361] *Manuscript Sources in the Library of Congress for Research on the American Revolution,* by John R. Sellers (Washington: Library of Congress, 1975). Includes both domestic collections and reproductions of foreign materials.

[362] *Manuscripts of the American Revolution in the Boston Public Library: A Descriptive Catalog* (Boston: G. K. Hall and Company, 1968).

[363] *North American Forest History: A Guide to Archives and Manuscripts in the United States and Canada,* by Richard C. Davis (Santa Barbara, Calif.: Clio Books, for the Forest History Society, 1977).

[364] *Women's History Sources: A Guide to Archives and Manuscript Collections in the United States,* by Andrea Hinding, 2 vols. (New York: R. R. Bowker Company, 1979). This monumental work provides in vol. 1 an annotated listing of 18,026 collections arranged geographically and in vol. 2 a detailed name, subject, and geographic index.

[365] *Spanish and Mexican Records of the American Southwest: A Bibliographical Guide to Archive and Manuscript Sources,* by Henry Putney Beers (Tucson: University of Arizona Press, 1979).

There are also published guides to the personal papers of historically important persons. These can usually be located in Hamer's *Guide to Archives and Manuscripts* [298], the *Directory of Archives and Manuscript Repositories* [300], or in biographical bibliographies.

Note that some scholarly historical journals regularly publish information on new accessions of manuscript material in given repositories.

Guides to Manuscripts on American History in Foreign Repositories

Although most manuscripts dealing with American history are in repositories in the United States, in some cases foreign manuscripts may be essential for a research topic. An early group of guides to such sources in British repositories was published in the early part of the twentieth century by the Carnegie Institution, Washington, D.C. Examples of more recent guides are the following:

[366] "Copies of French Manuscripts for American History in the Library of Congress," by James E. O'Neill, *Journal of American History* 51 (March 1965): 674–91.

[367] *European Manuscript Sources of the American Revolution,* by W. J. Koenig and S. L. Mayer (New York: R. R. Bowker Company, 1974).

[368] *Guide des sources de l'histoire des Etats-Unis dans les archives françaises* (Paris: France Expansion, 1976).

[369] *A Guide to Cherokee Documents in Foreign Archives,* by William L. Anderson and James A. Lewis (Metuchen, N.J.: Scarecrow Press, 1983).

[370] *A Guide to Manuscripts Relating to America in Great Britain and Ireland,* rev. ed., by John W. Raimo (Westport, Conn.: Meckler Books, for the British Association for American Studies, 1979). A revision of the 1961 guide by B. R. Crick and Miriam Alman.

[371] *Guide to Manuscripts Relating to American History in British Depositories Reproduced for the Division of Manuscripts of the Library of Congress,* by Grace Gardner Griffin (Washington: Library of Congress, 1946).

Calendars and Indexes

A great boon to researchers in manuscript collections are calendars and indexes. The first are the most help, for they identify each document in a collection (usually listed chronologically) and present a brief summary of the contents, and this material is sometimes indexed by person and subject. With a calendar in hand a researcher can quickly find the pertinent documents without having to read through all the documents in the collection. In fact, the first question a researcher should ask in approaching a manuscript collection is, "Does this collection have a calendar?"

Some collections have unpublished calendars in card catalog form. A few detailed calendars have been published, of which the following are good examples: [372] *Calendar of the American Fur Company's Papers,* by Grace Lee Nute, *Annual Report of the American Historical Association for the Year 1944,* vols. 2–3 (Washington: Government Printing Office, 1945); and [373] *Calendar of the Papers of Martin Van Buren,* by Elizabeth Howard West (Washington: Government Printing Office, 1910).

Some extensive manuscript collections have indexes, which provide a complete listing of the documents (in most cases chronologically, showing author and recipient of correspondence). The indexes do not give a summary of the contents of the documents, but they often enable a researcher to sort out possibly useful documents, even though many will have to be put aside if their contents are not pertinent. Among important published indexes are the Library of Congress's [374] *Presidents' Papers Index Series* (Washington: Manuscript Division, Library of Congress, 1960–1976). These are computer-generated indexes to the microfilm edition of the presidential papers in the Library of Congress. They list all the letters and other documents by correspondents and date. Twenty-three presidents are covered in the series: Washington, Jefferson, Madison, Monroe, Jackson, Van Buren, W. H. Harrison, Tyler, Polk, Taylor, Pierce, Lincoln, A. Johnson, Grant, Garfield, Arthur, Cleveland, B. Harrison, McKinley, T. Roosevelt, Taft, Wilson, and Coolidge.

9

Guides to Newspapers

Newspapers are a valuable and widely used source of information for American historians. They offer detailed chronological information of events, often on a day-to-day basis. They indicate the interests of the time by the priority they give to news events. Their editorials provide a view of opinion, and advertisements can be a source for social history. Many newspapers are important for the local news they supply. Newspapers, of course, must be used with caution, for biases frequently influence the selection of news as well as editorial comment. Accuracy, too, is a problem, for the pressures of daily publication prevent the kind of verification of facts that historians want. Yet, all in all, there are few topics that can dispense with newspaper sources, and for some subjects the newspapers may be the only source.

Bibliographies and Union Lists

The most important modern list of American newspapers is being produced by the United States Newspaper Program (USNP), begun in 1976 under the sponsorship of the Organization of American Historians and the Library of Congress, with grants from the National Endowment for the Humanities. The USNP is intended as a kind of clearing-house to promote state action in seeking out newspaper holdings and publishing bibliographies of them, in conservation of newspapers by microfilming, in preparation of descriptive cataloguing data for all newspapers, and in conversion of data to standardized machine-readable form so that there can be a single comprehensive database. The USNP is designed to identify all newspapers published in the United States and its Trust Territories, to identify repositories that collect those newspapers, and to list the holdings in those repositories.

The latest publication of the data is [376] *United States Newspaper Program National Union List,* 3d ed. (Dublin, Ohio: OCLC Online

Computer Library Center, 1989). The *National Union List* is derived from an online database of information entered by the repositories participating in the program. The participants are national repositories, which inventory and catalog newspapers accumulated according to their nationwide collection policies, and state projects, which locate and catalog newspapers in state and local repositories. The 3d edition of 1989 includes all newspaper data entered into the OCLC Online Union Catalog as of April 1989 by the Library of Congress; by the following national repositories: American Antiquarian Society, Center for Research Libraries, Kansas State Historical Society, New-York Historical Society, New York Public Library, Rutgers University, State Historical Society of Wisconsin, and Western Reserve Historical Society; by state projects in Alabama, Arkansas, Colorado, Delaware, Georgia, Hawaii, Idaho, Indiana, Iowa, Kentucky, Maryland, Massachusetts, Mississippi, Missouri, Montana, Nevada, New Jersey, New York, North Dakota, Ohio, Pennsylvania, Texas, Utah, Washington, West Virginia, and Wisconsin; and by Puerto Rico and the United States Virgin Islands.

The *United States Newspapers Program National Union List,* 3d ed., consists of 1) bibliographic records of the newspapers in an alphabetical list, 2) local data records that indicate the issues of a newspaper held by each repository, 3) a "Key to Institution Codes," which identifies the repositories, and 4) three indexes: beginning date–ending date (chronologically by earliest publication date), language (alphabetically by language), and place of publication/printing (alphabetically by state and city). The bibliographic records and the indexes are issued in microfiche; the "Key to Institution Codes" is in printed pamphlet form. The pamphlet and the microfiche in pockets are bound together in a single loose-leaf binder. The data are also available online from OCLC, but researchers will probably find the microfiche more convenient unless they are seeking information only on a specific newspaper.

While the USNP is in progress and even after it is finally completed, a history student will find it valuable and convenient to use other, older guides to American newspapers. There are two standard general compilations. The first is [377] *History and Bibliography of American Newspapers, 1690–1820*, by Clarence S. Brigham, 2 vols. (Worcester, Mass.: American Antiquarian Society, 1947), which is supplemented by [378] *Additions and Corrections to History and Bibliography of American Newspapers, 1690–1820* (Worcester, Mass.: American Antiquarian Society, 1961), reprinted from the *Proceedings of the American An-*

tiquarian Society, April 1961. Brigham's two volumes list 2,120 newspapers by state and town and indicate libraries that have holdings of the papers. They include a list of libraries, an index of titles, and an index of printers. The second guide, which continues Brigham, is an oversize volume, [379] *American Newspapers, 1821–1936: A Union List of Files Available in the United States and Canada,* by Winifred Gregory (New York: H. W. Wilson Company, 1937), which is similar in arrangement to Brigham's work. A work that to some extent parallels Brigham's and Gregory's volumes is [380] *History and Present Condition of the Newspaper and Periodical Press of the United States,* by S. N. D. North (Washington: Government Printing Office, 1884). It treats the subject by three chronological periods: 1639–1783, 1783–1835, and 1835–1880. See also the following guides to early American newspapers: [381] *Chronological Tables of American Newspapers, 1690–1820: Being a Tabular Guide to Holdings of Newspapers Published in America through the Year 1820,* by Edward Connery Lathem (Barre, Mass.: American Antiquarian Society and Barre Publishers, 1972), and [382] *Check List of American Eighteenth Century Newspapers in the Library of Congress,* rev. ed., by Henry S. Parsons (Washington: Government Printing Office, 1936), a work originally compiled by John Van Ness Ingram.

General directories of newspapers and periodicals can also be of use in tracking down newspaper sources. The *Gale Directory of Publications and Broadcast Media* [289] is a standard American list of currently published daily newspapers and is arranged alphabetically by state and city. It includes classified lists of agricultural, ethnic, and fraternal publications. See also *Newspapers in Microform* [415], discussed below.

State and Other Specialized Directories

Even when the United States Newspaper Program is completed, various state directories of newspapers may prove valuable to a researcher. Some of these are listed below. Most of them are union lists.

[383] *History and Bibliography of Alabama Newspapers in the Nineteenth Century,* by Rhoda Coleman Ellison (University, Ala.: University of Alabama Press, 1954).

[384] *A Guide to Alaska's Newspapers,* by Phyllis Davis (Juneau: Gastineau Channel Centennial Association and Alaska Division of State Libraries and Museums, 1976).

[385] *Newspapers and Periodicals of Arizona, 1859–1911*, by Estelle Lutrell, *University of Arizona Bulletin* 20 (July 1949).

[386] *Guide to Colorado Newspapers, 1859–1963*, by Donald E. Oehlerts (Denver: Bibliographical Center for Research, Rocky Mountain Region, 1964).

[387] *The Hawaiian Newspapers*, by Esther K. Mookini (Honolulu: Topgallant Publishing Company, 1974).

[388] "Newspapers in the Illinois State Historical Library," by William E. Keller, *Illinois Libraries* 49 (June 1967): 439–543.

[389] *A Bibliography of Iowa Newspapers, 1836–1976* (Iowa City: Iowa State Historical Department Division of the State Historical Society, 1979).

[390] *Louisiana Newspapers, 1794–1961: A Union List of Louisiana Newspaper Files Available in Public, College and University Libraries in Louisiana*, by T. N. McMullan (Baton Rouge: Library, Louisiana State University, 1965).

[391] *Missouri Newspapers: When and Where, 1808–1963*, by William H. Taft (Columbia: State Historical Society of Missouri, 1964).

[392] *A Guide to the Newspaper Collection of the State Archives, Nebraska State Historical Society*, by Anne P. Diffendal (Lincoln: Nebraska State Historical Society, 1977).

[393] *The Newspapers of Nevada: A History and Bibliography, 1854–1979*, by Richard E. Lingenfelter and Karen Rix Gash (Reno: University of Nevada Press, 1984).

[394] *Directory of New Jersey Newspapers, 1765–1970*, by William C. Wright and Paul A. Stellhorn (Trenton: New Jersey Historical Commission, 1977).

[395] *New Mexico Newspapers: A Comprehensive Guide to Bibliographical Entries and Locations*, by Pearce S. Grove, Becky J. Garnett, and Sandra J. Hansen (Albuquerque: University of New Mexico Press, in cooperation with Eastern New Mexico University, 1975).

[396] *Union List of North Carolina Newspapers, 1751–1900*, by H. G. Jones and Julius H. Avant (Raleigh, N.C.: State Department of Archives and History, 1963).

[397] *North Dakota Newspapers, 1864–1976: A Union List*, by Carol Koehmstedt Kolar (Fargo: North Dakota Institute for Regional Studies, 1981).

[398] *Guide to Ohio Newspapers, 1793–1973: Union Bibliography of*

Ohio Newspapers Available in Ohio Libraries, by Stephen Gutgesell (Columbus: Ohio Historical Society, 1974).

[399] *Pennsylvania Newspapers: A Bibliography and Union List,* 2d ed., by Glenora E. Rossell (Pittsburgh: Pennsylvania Library Association, 1978).

[400] *Tennessee Newspapers: A Cumulative List of Microfilmed Tennessee Newspapers in the Tennessee State Library* (Nashville: Tennessee State Library and Archives, 1978).

[401] *Virginia Newspapers, 1821–1935: A Bibliography with Historical Introduction and Notes,* by Lester J. Cappon (New York: D. Appleton-Century Company, 1936).

[402] *Guide to Wisconsin Newspapers, 1833–1957,* by Donald E. Oehlerts (Madison: State Historical Society of Wisconsin, 1958).

[403] *Wisconsin Newspapers, 1833–1850: An Analytical Bibliography,* by James L. Hansen (Madison: State Historical Society of Wisconsin, 1979).

[404] *Guide to Wyoming Newspapers, 1867–1967,* by Lola M. Homsher (Cheyenne: Wyoming State Library, 1971).

Checklists of state newspapers for Arkansas, Louisiana, Massachusetts, Mississippi, Pennsylvania, Texas, Utah, Vermont, and Wisconsin were prepared by the Historical Records Survey of the Work Projects Administration. See *Bibliography of Research Projects Reports* [190], pp. 73–74.

Other directories of newspapers pertain to local regions, to particular population groups, to specific libraries, or to special topics. Some examples of such lists are given here.

[405] *American Indian and Alaska Native Newspapers and Periodicals,* by Daniel F. Littlefield, Jr., and James W. Parins, 3 vols. (Westport, Conn.: Greenwood Press, 1984–1986). The volumes are divided as follows: 1826–1924, 1925–1970, 1971–1985.

[406] *The Black Press in Mississippi, 1865–1985: A Directory,* by Julius E. Thompson (West Cornwall, Conn.: Locust Hill Press, 1988).

[407] *Chinese Newspapers Published in North America, 1854–1975,* by Karl Lo and H. M. Lai (Washington: Center for Chinese Research Materials, Association of Research Libraries, 1977).

[408] *The College Media Directory,* 7th ed. (New York: Oxbridge Communications, 1980), formerly *Directory of the College Student Press in America.*

[409] *Encyclopedic Directory of Ethnic Newspapers and Periodicals in*

the United States, 2d ed., by Lubomyr R. Wynar and Anna T. Wynar (Littleton, Colo.: Libraries Unlimited, 1976).

[410] *Extant Collections of Early Black Newspapers: A Research Guide to the Black Press, 1880–1915, with an Index to the Boston Guardian, 1902–1904,* by Georgetta Merritt Campbell (Troy, N.Y.: Whitston Publishing Company, 1981).

[411] *Newspapers and Periodicals by and about Black People: Southeastern Library Holdings* (Boston: G. K. Hall and Company, 1978).

[412] *The People's Voice: An Annotated Bibliography of American Presidential Campaign Newspapers, 1828–1984,* by William Miles (Westport, Conn.: Greenwood Press, 1987).

[413] *A Register and History of Negro Newspapers in the United States, 1827–1950,* by Armistead S. Pride (Ann Arbor, Mich.: University Microfilms, 1973).

[414] *A Survey of Black Newspapers in America,* by Henry G. La Brie III (Kennebunkport, Me.: Mercer House Press, 1979).

Newspapers on Microfilm

A researcher using newspapers must be resigned to reading them on microfilm. Because of the problems of storage and of preservation, many newspaper files are now on microfilm. Even current national dailies like the *New York Times* are often kept on file by libraries only until the microfilm edition arrives. And for many older newspapers, which frequently are in a bad state of preservation, only microfilm copies are available. It is not easy to use microfilmed newspapers, especially early ones that have very small type, but without the microfilm the availability of these valuable sources would be greatly diminished.

The Catalog Management and Publication Division of the Library of Congress provides an extensive guide to microfilmed newspapers in [415] *Newspapers in Microform: United States, 1948–1983,* 2 vols. (Washington: Library of Congress, 1984). A number of the directories listed in the preceding sections also pertain to microfilm.

Newspaper Indexes

Research in newspapers is greatly facilitated by indexes to newspapers, which furnish a guide to persons and events. The most important of these is the [416] *New York Times Index* (New York: New York Times, 1913–), which appears semimonthly with annual cumulations. It is a detailed index to subject, persons, and organizations, and by supplying dates can be used as an index to other newspapers that are likely to have reported the same events. Although the current indexes began in 1913, retrospective indexes back to the beginning of the *New York Times* in 1851 have been published. The indexes themselves can be supplemented by [417] *Personal Names Index to "The New York Times Index," 1851–1974*, by Byron A. Falk, Jr., and Valerie R. Falk, 22 vols. (Succasunna, N.J.: Roxbury Data Interface, 1976–1983), which has a 5-volume supplement for 1975–1989 (1990–1991), and the *New York Times Obituaries Index* [496]. See also [418] *Guide to the Incomparable New York Times Index,* by Grant W. Morse (New York: Fleet Academic Editions, 1980).

Other newspapers of national circulation have indexes, but they began much later than that of the *New York Times*. There are printed indexes, for example, to the *Wall Street Journal,* the *Christian Science Monitor,* the *Chicago Tribune,* and the *Washington Post.* For a newspaper index that has ceased publication, see [419] *New York Daily Tribune Index, 1875–1906*, 31 vols. (New York: Tribune Association, 1876–1907).

A large number of newspapers are now indexed in machine-readable form and can be accessed online or on CD-ROM. Some of the newspaper services offer abstracts and others full text of news items and features as well as indexes, although these begin only in the 1980s or 1990s. Among the services that offer newspaper information are *Data Times,* a division of DATATEK Corporation; VU/TEXT, owned by the Knight-Ridder newspaper chain; *Data Courier,* a product of UMI/Data Courier; *National Newspaper Index,* of Information Access Company, the producer of InfoTrac CD-ROMs; NEXIS, of Mead Data Central; and *NewsBank Electronic Index.* Because of the rapidly changing status of these newspaper indexes, abstracts, and full-text presentations, it will be necessary to check with librarians to see what is up to date at a given time and what is available in the library in which the research is being done. Again, it seems wise to note that unless a historian needs very recent material, the newspapers now available in machine-readable form will not be of great use.

Besides the printed and electronic indexes to the large national dailies, there are published indexes for a number of local or regional papers and for papers of particular periods or subjects. A valuable index for the colonial period is [420] *Virginia Gazette Index, 1736–1780*, by Lester J. Cappon and Stella F. Duff, 2 vols. (Williamsburg, Va.: Institute of Early American History and Culture, 1950). For black newspapers, see [421] *Index to Black Newspapers,* begun in 1977 by the Newspaper Indexing Center of the Bell and Howell Company.

Some newspapers that do not have published indexes have card file indexes or other forms that can be used by researchers. An early guide to such indexes is [422] "Preliminary Guide to Indexed Newspapers in the United States, 1850–1900," by Herbert O. Brayer, *Mississippi Valley Historical Review* 33 (September 1946): 237–58. More recent and comprehensive is [423] *Lathrop Report on Newspaper Indexes: An Illustrated Guide to Published and Unpublished Newspaper Indexes in the United States and Canada,* by Norman M. Lathrop and Mary Lou Lathrop (Wooster, Ohio: Norman Lathrop Enterprises, 1979). Of use also is [424] *Newspaper Indexes: A Location and Subject Guide for Researchers,* by Anita Cheek Milner, 3 vols. (Metuchen, N.J.: Scarecrow Press, 1977–1982). A regional guide is [425] *A Guide to Newspaper Indexes in New England* (Holden, Mass.: Bibliography Committee, New England Library Association, 1978).

Newspaper Libraries

Information on repositories with organized collections of newspapers can be found in [426] *Newspaper Libraries in the U.S. and Canada: An SLA Directory,* 2d ed., by Elizabeth L. Anderson (New York: Special Libraries Association, 1980), and [427] *Newspaper Libraries: A Bibliography, 1933–1985,* by Celia Jo Wall (Washington: Special Libraries Association, 1986).

10

Lists and Abstracts of
Dissertations and Theses

Any serious researcher in American history topics must find a way
through the great mass of academic dissertations and theses, which contain much useful and otherwise unavailable information. Many of these
studies are published eventually in revised form as books or articles,
which in most cases then supersede the original work, but many more are
never published, and sometimes those that are published lack a full citation of sources. Dissertations and theses cover a wide variety of subjects,
often represent new approaches and new materials, and are heavily docu-
mented. As a whole they are a good indication of the current academic
work being done. A survey of recent dissertations and theses will dis-
close topics already preempted and perhaps also gaps yet to be filled.

Dissertation Abstracts

It is relatively easy to locate useful dissertations, for there is a convenient
compilation of abstracts and a comprehensive index. The place to begin
is [428] *Dissertation Abstracts International (DAI)* (Ann Arbor: University Microfilms, 1938–). Originally entitled *Microfilm Abstracts* and
then *Dissertation Abstracts,* this multivolume set provides abstracts of
dissertations submitted by cooperating universities, covering the period
1861 to the present. For each dissertation, in addition to the author and title, it supplies order number, university, date, name of supervisor, number of pages, and an abstract furnished by the author. The publication appears monthly and is divided into two sections, (A) *The Humanities and
Social Sciences* and (B) *The Sciences and Engineering.* A third section
(C) *Worldwide,* formerly *European Abstracts,* begun in 1976, covers dissertations submitted to foreign universities, chiefly those in Western Europe. This section appears quarterly and has an author index cumulated
annually.

To locate dissertations in *Dissertation Abstracts International,* use the [429] *Comprehensive Dissertation Index, 1861–1972*, 37 vols. (Ann Arbor: Xerox University Microfilms, 1973). The set is broken down by subject, with vol. 28 devoted to History; vols. 33–37 are an author index. This index seeks to list all dissertations accepted at universities in the United States for the period; some Canadian and other foreign universities are also included. There is a ten-year supplement, [430] *Comprehensive Dissertation Index Ten-Year Cumulation, 1973–1982*, 38 vols. (Ann Arbor: University Microfilms International, 1984), and a five-year supplement of 22 vols. for the years 1983 to 1987, published in 1989. Annual supplements appear between the multiyear cumulations.

There are a good many special subject bibliographies published by University Microfilms International (UMI), 20 to 40 pages in length, that are extracted from the full database and cover only a set number of years. These include such topics of interest to the researcher in United States history as black studies, sex in contemporary society, United States foreign relations, ecology and the environment, urban studies, women's studies, ethnic studies, urban problems, United States presidents, and the colonial and early national periods.

University Microfilms International, beginning in 1962, has also published [431] *Masters Abstracts International*, formerly called *Masters Abstracts: Abstracts of Selected Masters Theses on Microfilm*. Issued quarterly, it has become increasingly inclusive.

In addition, UMI publishes [432] *American Doctoral Dissertations*, which appears annually on an academic-year basis. It is arranged by subject category, institution, and author. Originally titled *Index to American Doctoral Dissertations*, covering the United States and Canada, it began in 1955–1956.

The entire *Dissertation Abstracts* database is available online and is now available also on CD-ROM as [433] *Dissertation Abstracts Ondisc*. It includes more than one million records on five discs. One covers over 600,000 titles, citations only, from 1861 to June 1980. Four other discs, for given periods of years, cover nearly 500,000 titles, including abstracts as well as the citations, from July 1980 to the present. The current disc is updated twice a year; some 40,000 titles are added annually. *Dissertation Abstracts Ondisc* includes the contents of *Dissertation Abstracts International* [428], Sections A, B, and C, *Comprehensive Dissertation Index* [429], *Masters Abstracts International* [431], and *American Doctoral Dissertations* [432]. While the discs are useful for detailed subject searches and can be searched also by author, institution, name of adviser, date, and language, the fact that abstracts appear only for titles from 1980 forward means that the printed volumes still remain a necessity.

Other Guides to Dissertations and Theses

In addition to the publications of University Microfilms International, there are other guides that may be of value. Two older lists are [434] *Doctoral Dissertations Accepted by American Universities,* compiled for the Association of Research Libraries, nos. 1–22 (New York: H. W. Wilson Company, 1934–1955), which runs from 1933–1934 through 1954–1955 and is arranged by subject and then university, with author index; and [435] *List of American Doctoral Dissertations Printed in* 1912 (–1938), 26 vols. (Washington: Government Printing Office, 1913–1940). The latter, prepared by the Catalog Division of the Library of Congress, provides an alphabetical author list of dissertations printed during each year, as well as an index of subjects and a list of dissertations by degree-granting institution.

Lists of doctoral dissertations that pertain specifically to history are useful, for they have sorted out historical dissertations from the large mass. The best is [436] *Dissertations in History: An Index to Dissertations Completed in History Departments of United States and Canadian Universities, 1873–1960,* by Warren F. Kuehl (Lexington: University of Kentucky Press, 1965). There are two supplements, also compiled by Kuehl: *1961–June 1970* (Lexington: University Press of Kentucky, 1972); and *1970–June 1980* (Santa Barbara, Calif.: ABC-Clio, 1985). These volumes include dissertations from *Dissertation Abstracts International* and also some not listed in that source. The items are classified by subject (subdivided by region and by chronological period) and indexed by author and subject. See also the American Historical Association's [437] *Doctoral Dissertations in History,* which began in 1909 and has had varying titles and publishers. Since 1947 it has been published in Washington by the Association; it is now published semiannually. Originally a list of dissertations in progress, since 1958 it has also included completed dissertations. The arrangement is by field of history; there are author indexes.

For more on masters theses, see [438] *Master's Theses in the Arts and Social Sciences,* 1976– (Cedar Falls, Iowa: Research Publications, 1977–). The theses (reported by graduate schools in the United States and

Canada) are arranged by subject categories. There is an institution index in each volume, and early volumes also had an author index. See also [439] *Guide to Lists of Master's Theses,* by Dorothy M. Black (Chicago: American Library Association, 1965). This volume provides general lists, lists of theses by subject matter, and lists by institutions, but it includes material only through 1964.

There are a great many publications that list dissertations and/or theses on particular topics or for specific geographical areas. A general guide to such works, international in scope, is [440] *A Guide to Theses and Dissertations: An International Bibliography of Bibliographies,* by Michael M. Reynolds, rev. and enl. ed. (Phoenix: Oryx Press, 1985). It is arranged by nation and by subject, with indexes of institutions, names and titles, and specific subjects; it includes both serial and one-time publications.

Many degree granting institutions from time to time issue lists of dissertations and theses submitted in their graduate programs. Some of these are one-time publications; others are ongoing series. And there are compilations of dissertations and theses that pertain to a particular state, city, or other geographical area.

A large number of bibliographies of dissertations have been compiled according to special topics. The following are some examples:

[441] *The American Indian in Graduate Studies: A Bibliography of Theses and Dissertations,* by Frederick J. Dockstader (New York: Museum of the American Indian, Heye Foundation, 1957), which covers the period 1890–1955. A second volume by Frederick J. Dockstader and Alice W. Dockstader, covering 1955–1970, was published by the Museum in 1974.

[442] *American Library History: A Bibliography of Dissertations and Theses,* by Arthur P. Young, 3d rev. ed. (Metuchen, N.J.: Scarecrow Press, 1988).

[443] *American Puritan Studies: An Annotated Bibliography of Dissertations, 1882–1981,* by Michael S. Montgomery (Westport, Conn.: Greenwood Press, 1984).

[444] *An Analysis of Public Policy: A Bibliography of Dissertations, 1977–1982,* by John S. Robey (Westport, Conn.: Greenwood Press, 1984).

[445] *Cities and Towns in American History: A Bibliography of Doctoral Dissertations,* by Arthur P. Young (Westport, Conn.: Greenwood Press, 1989).

[446] *Dissertations in the History of Education, 1970–1980*, by Edward R. Beauchamp (Metuchen, N.J.: Scarecrow Press, 1985).

[447] *Doctoral Dissertations in Military Affairs*, by Allan R. Millett and B. F. Cooling (Manhattan: Kansas State University Library, 1972).

[448] *Higher Education in American Life, 1636–1986: A Bibliography of Dissertations and Theses*, by Arthur P. Young (Westport, Conn.: Greenwood Press, 1988).

[449] *Immigrants and Their Children in the United States: A Bibliography of Doctoral Dissertations, 1885–1982*, by W. William Hoglund (New York: Garland Publishing, 1986).

[450] *Labor Relations and Collective Bargaining: A Bibliographic Guide to Doctoral Research*, by Milden J. Fox, Jr., and Patsy Cliffene Howard (Metuchen, N.J.: Scarecrow Press, 1983).

[451] *Native North Americans in Doctoral Dissertations, 1971–1975: A Classified Indexed Research Bibliography*, by Gifford S. Nickerson (Monticello, Ill.: Council of Planning Libraries, 1977).

[452] *Theses and Dissertations on Virginia History: A Bibliography*, by Richard R. Duncan (Richmond: Virginia State Library, 1985).

[453] *Women's Studies: A Bibliography of Dissertations, 1870–1982*, by V. F. Gilbert and D. S. Tatla (New York: Basil Blackwell, 1985). Lists doctoral dissertations from the United States and theses and dissertations from British, Canadian, and Irish universities.

Some scholarly journals and bibliographical publications print lists of dissertations that pertain to American history. Although these for the most part are merely selections from *Dissertation Abstracts International* [428], they are convenient places to find recent dissertations. See especially *America: History and Life* [111], which now adds dissertations to articles and book reviews under each subject heading, and the *Journal of American History*, which includes dissertations in the section "Recent Scholarship," arranged by subject.

11

Biographical Guides

Biographical sources offer tremendous riches for the researcher in United States history. The lives of important figures tell us much about historical events, and some historians argue that a biographical approach is the most effective way to present history. Certainly historical writing cannot easily come alive without attention to human actors.

Much information about men and women of the past can be located through general bibliographies. *Writings on American History* [105], for example, lists thousands of individuals in its citations, and nearly all historical bibliographies have a biographical element. Similarly, manuscript depositories classify a large proportion of their holdings by individual persons—both in designating collections and in indexing or calendaring the contents of the collections. The *National Union Catalog of Manuscript Collections* [296] and other guides to manuscripts are among the first places to look if one seeks to track down a historical personage.

There are, however, numerous reference works that are concerned specifically with biography. These include biographical dictionaries, which run from long biographical sketches to brief statements of vital statistics; they are useful in checking names, dates, and careers of individuals who enter into written histories. There are, in addition, lists of diaries, autobiographies, and biographies to aid the researcher in locating detailed information about persons from both the past and the present.

Indexes and Guides to Collective Biographies and Biographical Dictionaries

Unless the person for whom biographical information is sought is a historical figure of some prominence, who might appear in works like the *Dictionary of American Biography* [463] it is best to begin one's search with a master list of biographical entries in dictionaries and works of collective biography. Such lists direct the researcher to published biographical dictionaries and other such works that contain the person looked for, which then can be searched for the needed biographical data. The largest such master list is [454] *Biography and Genealogy Master Index: A Consolidated Index to More Than 3,200,000 Biographical Sketches in Over 350 Current and Retrospective Biographical Dictionaries (BGMI)*, 2d ed., by Miranda C. Herbert and Barbara McNeil, 8 vols. (Detroit: Gale Research Company, 1980). Supplements have been published to cover the years 1981–1992. The base set and its eleven supplements index a total number of biographical sketches that exceeds 8,383,000. A similar work from the same database, published in microfiche, is [455] *Bio-Base: A Master Index on Microfiche to More Than 7,482,000 Biographical Sketches Found in Over 600 Current and Retrospective Biographical Dictionaries,* 1990 Master Cumulation (Detroit: Gale Research, 1989). A majority of the sources indexed in *Bio-Base* cover individuals in the United States, but some sources cover individuals in foreign countries. The 1990 Master Cumulation has annual supplements, and a new cumulation is planned for 1995. The *Biography and Genealogy Master Index* is also available online as [456] *Biography Master Index (BMI)*.

Selected material from the *Biography and Genealogy Master Index* is found in [457] *Author Biographic Master Index: A Consolidated Index to More Than 845,000 Biographical Sketches Concerning Authors Living and Dead As They Appear in a Selection of the Principal Biographical Dictionaries Devoted to Authors, Poets, Journalists, and Other Literary Figures,* 3d ed., by Barbara McNeil, 2 vols. (Detroit: Gale Research, 1989); and [458] *Historical Biographical Dictionaries Master Index: A Consolidated Index to Biographical Information Concerning Historical Personages in Over 35 of the Principal Retrospective Biographical Dictionaries,* by Barbara McNeil and Miranda C. Herbert (Detroit: Gale Research Company, 1980).

A broad index is [459] *Analytical Bibliography of Universal Collected Biography, Comprising Books Published in the English Tongue in Great Britain and Ireland, America and the British Dominions,* by Phyllis M. Riches (London: Library Association, 1934; reprint, Detroit: Gale Research Company, 1980), which attempts to index every work of collected biography in English published before 1933. It includes some 56,000 names.

There are also simple bibliographies of biographical dictionaries and similar works. A comprehensive bibliography with about 4,800 entries, whose long subtitle describes its contents, is [460] *Bibliographical Dictionaries and Related Works: An International Bibliography of Collective Biographies, Biobibliographies, Collections of Epitaphs, Selected Genealogical Works, Dictionaries of Anonyms and Pseudonyms, Historical and Specialized Dictionaries, Biographical Materials in Government Manuals, Bibliographies of Biography, Biographical Indexes, and Selected Portrait Catalogs,* 2d ed., by Robert B. Slocum (Detroit: Gale Research Company, 1985). The [461] *ARBA Guide to Biographical Dictionaries,* by Bohdan S. Wynar (Littleton, Colo.: Libraries Unlimited, 1986), cumulates entries for 718 biographical dictionaries from past volumes of *American Reference Books Annual* [10] and describes, evaluates, and compares the works. A similar publication that contains older works as well as recent ones is [462] *Biographical Sources: A Guide to Dictionaries and Reference Works,* by Diane J. Cimbala, Jennifer Cargill, and Brian Alley (Phoenix: Oryx Press, 1986), which has 687 entries.

Comprehensive Works on American Biography

If one is dealing with a person of some importance in United States history, the best place to begin is the [463] *Dictionary of American Biography,* edited by Allen Johnson and Dumas Malone, 20 vols and Index (New York: Charles Scribner's Sons, 1928–1936). The work, published under the auspices of the American Council of Learned Societies, is generally known as the *DAB.* The articles in the *DAB,* which vary in length from about 500 to 16,500 words, are signed by the authors. They are authoritative and well written, and each includes bibliographical references. The index to the volumes lists persons by birthplace, occupation, and schools attended and includes lists of contributors and the biographical sketches each has written; no living persons were included. Eight supplements have been published from time to time (1944–1988) to add biographies of persons who have died. Supplement Eight brings the total coverage of the *DAB* to 18,100 sketches. There also is a [464] *Dictionary of American Biography Comprehensive Index* (New York: Charles Scribner's Sons, 1990), which covers entries in a ten-volume reprint of 1946 plus the eight supplements.

A [465] *Concise Dictionary of American Biography,* 4th ed. (New York: Charles Scribner's Sons, 1990), includes in one volume all the individuals in the original edition and the supplements but, of course, with greatly reduced entries. It is a convenient reference to have on hand if the multivolume edition is not immediately available.

A companion work to the *DAB,* constructed on the same pattern, is [466] *Notable American Women, 1607–1950: A Biographical Dictionary,* edited by Edward T. James and Janet Wilson James, 3 vols. (Cambridge: Harvard University Press, 1971). It contains biographical sketches of more than 1,350 women, most of whom are not included in the *DAB.* This original work has been supplemented by [467] *Notable American Women, the Modern Period: A Biographical Dictionary,* edited by Barbara Sicherman and Carol Hurd Green (Cambridge: Harvard University Press, 1980). Biographies of 442 women who died 1951–1975 are included in this volume.

A new work, intended to supersede the *DAB* and *Notable American Women,* is in progress: [468] *American National Biography,* under the general editorship of John A. Garraty, to be published in 20 volumes by Oxford University Press. It will contain newly written sketches of approximately 20,000 persons, and under consideration for inclusion are all persons in the *DAB, Notable American Women,* and other biographical collections. But a search is being made for other important persons whose careers have not been described in these publications.

In addition to the works just described, there are a number of older series. A more comprehensive one than the *DAB* and *Notable American Women* but less authoritatively done, with unsigned articles and no bibliographical references, is [469] *The National Cyclopaedia of American Biography,* (New York: J. T. White and Company, 1898–1984). There are two series, a permanent series of 62 numbered volumes and a current series of lettered volumes, A to M, (which began in 1930 and includes living persons only). A final volume, N-63, published in 1984, contains both permanent and current material. The volumes are not arranged alphabetically, so the general indexes are essential. The latest is [470] *Index: The National Cyclopaedia of American Biography* (Clifton, N.J.: James T. White and Company, 1984), which supersedes all previous indexes. This index is computer generated and covers the main biographical articles and also names, institutions, events, and other subjects mentioned in the articles. It covers all volumes published in both series.

A nineteenth-century biographical dictionary is [471] *Appleton's Cyclopaedia of American Biography,* edited by James Grant Wilson and John Fiske, 7 vols. (New York: D. Appleton and Company, 1887–1900). It includes native and naturalized citizens of the United States up to the time of compilation, plus some other eminent persons. Under each family name individual persons are arranged chronologically not alphabetically. There are small portraits of many individuals and many facsimiles of autographs. The work is not completely accurate, for some fictitious biographies slipped in. A supplementary volume is [472] *Notable Names in American History: A Tabulated Register* (Clifton, N.J.: James T. White and Company, 1973), which is a third edition of *White's Conspectus of American Biography* (1937). It includes chronological lists of officeholders of various kinds, such as presidents, cabinet members, governors of states, church leaders, and prize winners.

An ambitious microfiche publication project is [473] *American Biographical Archive,* managing ed. Laureen Baillie and ed. Gerry Easter (New York: K. G. Saur, 1986–1990), which reproduces on about 1,850 microfiche the printed sketches from 367 biographical reference works published between 1702 and 1920. About 300,000 individuals are included, with the various sketches cumulated in one alphabetical sequence. An *Index* to accompany the microfiche was published in 4 volumes in 1990. It includes basic biographical information and a listing of source works in which entries on each person appear.

Retrospective biographies appear also in the volumes of *Who Was Who in America* [485] and in *Who Was Who in America: Historical Volume, 1607–1896* [486].

Of considerable use for ready reference are a number of one-volume biographical dictionaries dealing with American history. See [474] *Webster's American Biographies,* edited by Charles Van Doren (Springfield, Mass.: Merriam-Webster, 1984), and [475] *Encyclopedia of American Biography,* edited by John A. Garraty and Jerome L. Sternstein (New York: Harper and Row, 1974). General and special one-volume encyclopedias of American history usually include biographical entries.

For an extensive bibliography of biographical information dealing with 6,000 Americans, see [476] *People in History: An Index to U.S. and Canadian Biographies in History Journals and Dissertations,* by Susan K. Kinnell, 2 vols. (Santa Barbara, Calif.: ABC-Clio, 1988), which cumulates biographical entries from *America: History and Life* [111] for the previous ten years. The [477] *Research Guide to American Historical Biography,* 5 vols. (Washington: Beacham Publishing, 1988–1991), provides biographical information and describes and evaluates important secondary and primary sources for 452 American historical figures.

Each entry is written by a specialist; the first three volumes were edited by Robert Muccigrosso.

Current Guides

For researching topics in the recent past or in the present, current indexes and biographical dictionaries that include living persons are necessary. An ongoing index is [478] *Biography Index: A Quarterly Index to Biographical Materials in Books and Magazines,* 1946– (New York: H. W. Wilson Company, 1949–), which indexes biographical material in works in English. There are annual and biennial cumulative volumes. Like other Wilson indexes, it is available online and on CD-ROM.

The most widely used compilation of biographical sketches of living persons is [479] *Who's Who in America,* 2 vols., now published in New Providence, N.J., by Marquis Who's Who. It is issued biennially, and its standards for entry are high. The intention is to provide biographies of the "best-known men and women in all lines of useful and reputable achievement," including (1) those chosen for special prominence in their fields and (2) those included on account of their official positions. The 1992–1993 edition contains entries for about 80,500 persons and provides also the names of persons listed in the regional editions. These regional volumes, published by Marquis Who's Who in Wilmette, Illinois, are listed here with the date they began; they are in general issued biennially. Canadian entries were added beginning with vol. 9 (1965–1966).
[480] *Who's Who in the East* (1948–). Includes eastern Canada.
[481] *Who's Who in the Midwest* (1949–). Includes central Canada.
[482] *Who's Who in the South and Southwest* (1950–). Includes Puerto Rico, the Virgin Islands, and Mexico.
[483] *Who's Who in the West* (1949–). Includes western Canada.

For a general current index, see [484] *Marquis Who's Who: Index to Who's Who Books, 1991* (Wilmette, Ill.: Marquis Who's Who, 1991), which contains the names of approximately 260,000 individuals included in *Who's Who in America* and the various regional and special group editions.

A related work, which includes persons dropped from the current *Who's Who* because of death, is [485] *Who Was Who in America,* 9 vols. to date, with coverage now from 1897 to 1989. In addition to these volumes, which take their entries from *Who's Who in America,* there is [486] *Who Was Who in America: Historical Volume, 1607–1896,* rev. ed.

(Chicago: Marquis Who's Who, 1967), which contains sketches of 13,250 individuals. A [487] *Who Was Who in America with World Notables: Index, 1607–1989* (Wilmette, Ill.: Marquis Who's Who, 1989), covers the historical volume and the 9 volumes published to date. Marquis also publishes bibliographical dictionaries dealing with selected groups of persons; a current list can be found opposite the title page in the latest edition of *Who's Who in America*.

An extensive compilation of biographical sketches is [488] *Current Biography* (New York: H. W. Wilson Company, 1940–), a monthly publication with bound annual cumulations entitled [489] *Current Biography Yearbook*. Between 300 and 350 biographies are printed annually. The biographical sketches are of persons of various nationalities, professions, and occupations who are prominent in their fields. Portraits and bibliographical references are included. A cumulated index appears in each annual volume, and separate indexes appear from time to time. See also [490] *Newsmakers: The People behind Today's Headlines* (Detroit: Gale Research, 1988–), a quarterly with annual cumulations formerly called *Contemporary Newsmakers* (1985–1987).

Biographical material from the *New York Times* is compiled monthly in [491] *The New York Times Biographical Service: A Compilation of Current Biographical Information of General Interest,* 1970–. The original title, vols. 1–5, was *New York Times Biographical Edition,* and the publisher varies; the work is now published by University Microfilms International in Ann Arbor, Mich. The work reproduces major biographical articles, both news-oriented biographical sketches and obituaries, usually with portraits or other illustrations. See also *Personal Names Index to "The New York Times Index," 1851–1974* [417].

For academic persons not in the sciences, see [492] *Directory of American Scholars: A Biographical Directory,* 8th ed., edited by the Jaques Cattell Press (New York: R. R. Bowker Company, 1982). Four volumes cover (1) history; (2) English, speech, and drama; (3) foreign languages, linguistics, and philology; and (4) philosophy, religion, and law. The first edition appeared in 1942. Related works by the same publisher are [493] *American Men and Women of Science: Social and Behavioral Sciences,* 13th ed., edited by Jaques Cattell Press (New York: R. R. Bowker Company, 1978); and [494] *American Men and Women of Science: A Biographical Directory of Today's Leaders in Physical, Biological, and Related Sciences,* 18th ed., 1992–1993, 8 vols. (New Providence, N.J.: R. R. Bowker, 1992). Vol. 8 is an index arranged by disciplines. Begun in 1906 as *American Men of Science,* the work has profiled more than 300,000 scientists and engineers in its 86-year history. The 18th edition alone lists 122,817 engineers and scientists; it is available online and on CD-ROM.

Obituaries

An obituary from a newspaper is sometimes the only or the fullest source about a person, and guides to such notices are important for the historical researcher seeking biographical information. There are a number of reference works to aid in the search.

The most comprehensive and useful is [495] *The New York Times Obituaries Index, 1858–1968* (New York: New York Times, 1970). It lists 353,000 names with references to the original news story in the *New York Times*. A ten-year supplement, [496] *The New York Times Obituaries Index, 1969–1978* (New York, 1980), adds some 36,000 persons and provides addenda and errata for the first volume. Reprints of some *New York Times* obituaries appear in the *New York Times Biographical Service* [491].

Obituaries for persons who have died in recent decades are gathered together in [497] *Obituaries on File,* compiled by Felice D. Levy, 2 vols. (New York: Facts on File, 1979). These volumes print in alphabetical order the brief obituary notices from *Facts on File* from its origin in 1940 through 1978. An index is included in vol. 2. A new annual series began with [498] *The Annual Obituary* 1980 (New York: St. Martin's Press, 1981), which includes obituaries of the world's notable people who died during the year. Later volumes have been published in Chicago by St. James Press; editors vary. Another new annual is [499] *Obituary Index,* 1988– (Westport, Conn.: Meckler, 1989–), which indexes obituaries in the *Atlantic Constitution, Boston Globe, Chicago Tribune, Los Angeles Times, New York Times,* the *Times* (London), and *Washington Post*.

See also [500] *Obituaries: A Guide to Sources,* by Betty M. Jarboe, 2d ed. (Boston: G. K. Hall and Company, 1989). This volume of some 3,550 entries lists a wide variety of specialized obituary publications. Those for the United States are listed by state.

Biographies, Autobiographies, and Diaries

Biographical dictionaries, the *Who's Whos,* and other collected biographies usually supply only brief sketches of individuals' lives. Fuller information is found in full-length biographies, in autobiographies, and in diaries, memoirs, and journals of important historical figures. For most of these materials, there are guides which will shorten the researcher's task.

Comprehensive inventories are [501] *Biographical Books, 1876–1949* (New York: R. R. Bowker Company, 1983), and [502] *Biographical Books, 1950–1980* (New York: R. R. Bowker Company, 1980). These volumes contain titles, extracted from the *American Book Publishing Record* [177], relating to biographies, autobiographies, diaries, and other biographical works. There are indexes arranged according to name/subject, occupations, authors, titles, and biographical books in print, but there are a good many duplicated entries. A useful work, though limited in scope and not up to date, is [503] *Guide to American Biography,* by Marion Dargan, 2 vols. (Albuquerque: University of New Mexico Press, 1949–1952). The first volume covers the dates 1607–1815, the second, 1815–1933. For each person there are references to original sources, to separately published studies, and to sketches in collected biographical works. More inclusive is the list of more than 2,200 individuals in the *Harvard Guide to American History* [114], pp. 156–274, which indicates important biographies and publications of the individuals' writings.

[504] *Biography by Americans, 1658–1936: A Subject Bibliography,* by Edward H. O'Neill (Philadelphia: University of Pennsylvania Press, 1939), tries to list all biographies written by Americans. The entries are arranged alphabetically by the subjects of the biographies. The volume lists 707 collective biographies in the second part of the book.

Autobiographies increase the wealth of information about historical individuals, adding a personal element not possible in biographies written by others. [505] *A Bibliography of American Autobiographies,* by Louis Kaplan (Madison: University of Wisconsin Press, 1961), has 6,377 entries arranged alphabetically by author, and there is also a subject index. A companion volume is [506] *American Autobiography, 1945–1980: A Bibliography,* by Mary Louise Briscoe (Madison: University of Wisconsin Press, 1982). A more limited work, which lists some 400 works published in 1900 or later, is [507] *American Life in Autobiogra-*

phy: A Descriptive Guide, by Richard G. Lillard (Stanford, Calif.: Stanford University Press, 1956). It lists entries alphabetically by occupation or profession, but there is also a general index. The author provides limited annotations.

Women's autobiographies are listed in [508] *Through a Woman's I: An Annotated Bibliography of American Women's Autobiographical Writings, 1946–1976,* by Patricia K. Addis (Metuchen, N.J.: Scarecrow Press, 1983), and [509] *First Person Female American: A Selected and Annotated Bibliography of the Autobiographies of American Women Living after 1950,* edited by Carolyn H. Rhodes (Troy, N.Y.: Whitston Publishing Company, 1980). For American Indians, see [510] *An Annotated Bibliography of American Indian and Eskimo Autobiographies,* by H. David Brumble III (Lincoln: University of Nebraska Press, 1981).

To biographies and autobiographies must be added diaries. A guide to early published diaries is [511] *American Diaries: An Annotated Bibliography of American Diaries Written Prior to the Year 1861,* by William Matthews with the assistance of Roy Harvey Pearce (Berkeley: University of California Press, 1945). Two works expand and revise Matthews's study. One is [512] *American Diaries: An Annotated Bibliography of Published American Diaries and Journals,* by Laura Arksey, Nancy Pries, and Marcia Reed, 2 vols. (Detroit: Gale Research Company, 1983–1987). Volume 1 covers the period 1492 to 1844; volume 2, 1845 to 1980. The other is [513] *And So to Bed: A Bibliography of Diaries Published in English,* by Patricia Pate Havlice (Metuchen, N.J.: Scarecrow Press, 1987). It is arranged chronologically and includes British and Canadian diaries. Manuscript diaries are listed in *American Diaries in Manuscript, 1580–1954* [345]. See also [514] *New England Diaries, 1602–1800: Descriptive Catalogue of Diaries, Orderly Books, and Sea Journals,* by Harriette Merrifield Forbes (Topsfield, Mass.: Privately printed, 1923); [515] *Guide to Mormon Diaries and Autobiographies,* by Davis Bitton (Provo: Brigham Young University Press, 1977), which gives full annotations for 2,894 manuscript and printed works; and [516] *The Published Diaries and Letters of American Women: An Annotated Bibliography,* by Joyce D. Goodfriend (Boston: G. K. Hall and Company, 1987).

Special Guides

A researcher may need to supplement the general biographical guides, both retrospective and current, with specialized guides or collections. A great number of these exist; in fact, hardly any historically important group of individuals has not been provided with some collective biographical publication. Works can be found for such diverse groups, for example, as African Americans, American Indians, journalists, political men and women, clergy, actors, musicians, artists, writers, labor leaders, religious figures, military officers, scientists, federal and state officials, Loyalists in the American Revolution, librarians, the federal judiciary, and women. There are also a good many separate bibliographies devoted specifically to an individual of historical importance, mostly political figures. For example, the Meckler Publishing Corporation is publishing a 50-volume series called [517] *Bibliographies of the Presidents of the United States,* which will include a bibliographical volume or volumes for each president from Washington to Reagan. When the series is completed a cumulated index will be issued in printed form and on CD-ROM. A similar series under way is the [518] *Twentieth Century Presidential Bibliography Series,* published by Scholarly Resources.

Of some use, especially for researchers in early American history, are the detailed alumni directories published by a number of colleges and universities for their early graduates. Among the most important of these are those for Harvard, Yale, and Princeton.

Many states and counties have biographical directories. Some of the volumes are vanity publications in which subscribers were written up; others are more scholarly efforts sponsored by historical societies or other such institutions.

Genealogy

A recent phenomenon is a tremendous interest in genealogy or "family history," as it is frequently designated. This search for one's family roots has brought to many persons a new interest in the past. Since the search is for one's ancestors, not specifically for historically significant persons, genealogy is not immediately of use to the historical researcher, but it may on occasion have a place. There are numerous guides to genealogical materials, including extensive genealogical indexes. Many of these are listed and annotated in *Guide to Reference Books* [8] and in *Craft of Public History* [14].

12

Oral History Materials

Interviews, both with historically important persons and with representatives of a variety of social and economic groups, are a valuable source for the historian. There were some early oral history programs, such as those conducted by Grant Foreman or Lyman C. Draper and those of the WPA, but it is in recent times that oral history has become a widely used technique. An important impetus came from Allan Nevins at Columbia University, who launched an oral history project there in 1948. The easy availability of tape recorders, of course, has helped make the new technique feasible.

Oral history collections contain interviews with politically significant persons, and leaders in business, religion, and other fields, too, have been sought out for interviews. But oral history has been especially helpful in gaining information about groups in American society who ordinarily leave little in the way of formal written records. Thus there are numerous studies that rely specifically on interviews and that include the phrase "an oral history" in their titles—about veterans of recent American wars; African Americans, American Indians, Hispanics, and other ethnic groups; laborers and those who live in rural areas; participants in civil rights movements; survivors of the Holocaust; the homeless; and various categories of American women.

The importance of oral history has been recognized by the Organization of American Historians, whose quarterly, the *Journal of American History,* since 1987 has included annually in the September issue a section on oral history. The section offers essays about specific oral history programs and examples of projects as well as an occasional article dealing with oral history in general. Two articles of special interest are [519] "On Using Oral History Collections: An Introduction," by Ronald J. Grele, *Journal of American History* 74 (September 1987): 570–78, which gives an overview of various oral history collections and describes access to them; and [520] "Oral History: Playing by the Rules," by David M. Oshinsky, *Journal of American History* 77 (September 1990):

609–14, which discusses proper procedures and reprints the American Historical Association's "Statement on Interviewing for Historical Documentation," a part of the Association's "Statement on Standards of Professional Conduct."

Guides and Manuals

Researchers in recent history may themselves decide to record interviews with participants in the events studied. To do this effectively, they can draw on the accumulated experience of others, set down in a number of useful manuals. Some of the following works describe techniques of interviewing and transcribing and will aid a beginning oral historian. Some of the more recent ones deal also with theoretical aspects of oral history and oral tradition.

[521] *Envelopes of Sound: The Art of Oral History,* edited by Ronald J. Grele, 2d ed., rev. (Chicago: Precedent Publishing, 1982). A series of essays and case studies.

[522] *From Memory to History: Using Oral Sources in Local Historical Research,* by Barbara Allen and William Lynwood Montell (Nashville: American Association for State and Local History, 1981).

[523] *Interviewing the People of Pennsylvania: A Conceptual Guide to Oral History* (Harrisburg: Pennsylvania Historical and Museum Commission, 1978). Describes a "grass roots" approach to oral history.

[524] *Listening to History: The Authenticity of Oral Evidence,* by Trevor Lummis (Totowa, N.J.: Barnes and Noble Books, 1987).

[525] *Oral Historiography,* by David Henige (New York: Longman, 1982).

[526] *Oral History: An Introduction for Students,* by James Hoopes (Chapel Hill: University of North Carolina Press, 1979).

[527] *Oral History: From Tape to Type,* by Cullom Davis, Kathryn Back, and Kay MacLean (Chicago: American Library Association, 1977).

[528] *Oral History and the Law,* by John N. Neuenschwander (Denton, Tex.: Oral History Association, 1985). A pamphlet that deals with legal issues in oral history and how to prevent legal problems.

[529] *Oral History for the Local Historical Society,* by Willa K. Baum, 3d ed., rev. (Nashville: American Association for State and Local History, 1987).

[530] *Oral History Program Manual,* by William W. Moss (New York: Praeger Publishers, 1974). Based on the oral history program of the John F. Kennedy Library.

[531] *Transcribing and Editing Oral History,* by Willa K. Baum (Nashville: American Association for State and Local History, 1977).

[532] *The Voice of the Past: Oral History,* by Paul Thompson, 2d ed. (New York: Oxford University Press, 1988). Deals with both theory and practical techniques.

[533] *Women's Words: The Feminist Practice of Oral History,* edited by Sherna Berger Gluck and Daphne Patai (New York: Routledge, 1991).

Bibliographies

As a growing field, oral history has spawned a considerable literature. There is an extensive annotated list of works dealing with oral history in *The Craft of Public History* [14], pp. 351–417. See also special bibliographies such as these: [534] *Bibliography on Oral History,* by Manfred J. Waserman, rev. ed. (Denton, Tex.: Oral History Association, 1975); and [535] *Oral History: A Reference Guide and Annotated Bibliography,* by Patricia Pate Havlice (Jefferson, N.C.: McFarland and Company, 1985).

General Directories

As the number of oral history programs has multiplied, directories have been prepared that describe the various programs and list persons and topics for which interviews are available. Two older works are [536] *Oral History in the United States: A Directory,* by Gary L. Shumway (New York: Oral History Association, 1971), which arranges oral history programs by state; and [537] *Oral History Collections,* by Alan M. Mechler and Ruth McMullin (New York: R. R. Bowker Company, 1975), an international directory of oral history centers, with a name and subject index. More recent works are the following:

[538] *Directory of Oral History Programs in the United States* (Sanford, N.C.: Microfilming Corporation of America, 1982).

[539] *Directory of Oral History Collections,* by Allen Smith (Phoenix: Oryx Press, 1988), which is arranged alphabetically by state, with a subject index.

[540] *Oral History Index: An International Directory of Oral History Interviews* (Westport, Conn.: Meckler, 1990), which provides an alphabetical index of more than 30,000 oral history transcripts in nearly 400 oral history centers in the United States, Canada, Great Britain, and Israel.

Particular Collections

In addition to the general directories, there are directories or catalogs that pertain to particular oral history collections. Some of these are state and regional compilations; a good many others describe the holdings of university oral history centers; still others deal with specific groups or topics. The following are some examples:

[541] *Catalogue of the Memoirs of the William E. Wiener Oral History Library* (New York: American Jewish Committee, 1978).

[542] *Catalogue of the Regional Oral History Office, 1954–1979,* by Suzanne B. Riess and Willa K. Baum (Berkeley: Regional Oral History Office, Bancroft Library, University of California, 1980).

[543] *A Directory of Oral History Interviews Related to the Federal Courts,* by Anthony Champagne, Cynthia Harrison, and Adam Land (Washington: Federal Judicial History Office, Federal Judicial Center, 1992).

[544] *A Guide to the Collections, 1970–85, Baylor University Institute for Oral History,* by Rebecca Sharpless Jimenez (Waco, Tex.: Baylor University, 1985).

[545] *A Guide to the Oral History Collection, Texas A & M University,* by Terry H. Anderson (College Station, Tex.: University Archives, Texas A & M University, 1988).

[546] *The Oral History Collection of Columbia University,* by Elizabeth Mason and Louis M. Starr (New York: Oral History Research Office, Columbia University, 1979). Because Columbia University was a pioneer in oral history, its collection is of special importance.

[547] *Oral History Collections in the Southwest Region: A Directory and Subject Guide,* by Cathryn A. Gallacher (Los Angeles: Southwest Oral History Association, 1986).

[548] *The Oral History Collections of the Minnesota Historical Society,* by Lila Johnson Goff and James E. Fogerty (St. Paul: Minnesota Historical Society Press, 1984).

[549] *The UCLA Oral History Program: Catalog of the Collection,* by Constance S. Bullock and Saundra Taylor (Los Angeles: Oral History Program, University of California, Los Angeles, 1982).

[550] *U.S. Naval Institute Oral History Collection: Catalog of Transcripts* (Annapolis: United States Naval Institute, 1983).

Oral history materials appear in a variety of general bibliographical reference works, identified by collection and in some cases by individual interview. Thus, for example, the Columbia University Oral History Program has produced machine-readable records for its holdings and has entered them into the online database of RLIN. Directories of manuscript collections often note oral history transcripts (see, for example, the *National Union Catalog of Manuscript Collections* [296], which beginning in 1970 has listed both interview transcripts and sound recordings).

Commercial publishers have made available some oral history material on microfiche. An important instance of this is The New York Times Oral History Program undertaken in the 1970s by Microfilming Corporation of America, which issued transcripts from the Columbia University Oral History Program and dozens of other important collections. Two issues of [551] *Oral History Guide* (No. 1 in 1976 and No. 2 in 1979) list the individual entries in the collections thus published. For some years Meckler Publishing issued on microfiche the Columbia University interviews, but it recently has sold its holdings to the Columbia University Oral History Research Office. Microfiche now available are listed in [552] *Columbia University Oral History Microfiche Collection: A Cumulative Index to Memoirs in Parts I-VI,* published by the Trustees of Columbia University of the City of New York.

Periodicals

To keep up to date in this fast-moving field, a researcher may need to refer to serial publications that note new oral history projects and developments in technique. An annual is [553] *The Oral History Review,* 1973–, published by the Oral History Association; it succeeds the [554] *National Colloquium on Oral History,* which provided transcriptions of the annual conferences of the Association, beginning in 1966. The journal [555] *Oral History* is the annual report of the Oral History Research Office, Columbia University. Although it deals with only one program, it provides good insights into the developing field of oral history. A new annual, which offers essays by different authors on oral history projects and problems is [556] *International Annual of Oral History,* 1990–, edited by Ronald J. Grele (New York: Greenwood Press, 1992–); it replaces the *International Journal of Oral History,* which began publication in 1980.

13

Printed Documents of the Federal Government

The federal government of the United States has entered into all aspects of American history, and its voluminous published documents are an extremely rich source of material for researchers in United States history. This is obviously true for political history and for such closely related areas as diplomatic, military, and legal history. But it is true also for broader areas of the nation's cultural history, for congressional action touches many subjects. There are very few topics for which historians can safely disregard federal records. It is important, then, that researchers know how to find their way confidently through the great bulk and maze of the records.

What is needed, first of all, is a thorough acquaintance with a general guide to printed government records. By far the best of these for the historian is still [557] *Government Publications and Their Use,* by Laurence F. Schmeckebier and Roy B. Eastin, 2d rev. ed. (Washington: Brookings Institution, 1969), now somewhat out of date. The book intelligently discusses the general catalogs and indexes to government publications, notes the availability of documents, and describes from a user's standpoint the various categories of congressional, executive, and judicial publications. There are special sections on state laws, administrative regulations, presidential papers, foreign affairs, reports on operations, and available maps. A detailed index adds to the usefulness of the work. A more recent guide, written chiefly for documents librarians, is [558] *Introduction to United States Public Documents,* by Joe Morehead, 3d ed. (Littleton, Colo.: Libraries Unlimited, 1983). Some of its technical discussion may frighten beginning researchers away, but the book is useful for looking up particular titles or specific points.

A listing of federal government publications is [559] *Government Reference Books 90/91: A Biennial Guide to U.S. Government Publications,* by LeRoy C. Schwarzkopf (Englewood, Colo.: Libraries Unlimited, 1992). See also [560] *A Bibliography of United States Government Bibliographies, 1968–1973,* by Roberta A. Scull (Ann Arbor, Mich.:

Pierian Press, 1975), and a supplementary volume covering the years 1974–1976 (1979). There is also [561] *Cumulative Subject Guide to U.S. Government Bibliographies, 1924–1973*, by Edna A. Kanely, 6 vols. (Arlington, Va.: Carrollton Press, 1976), to which has been added a 7th vol., [562] *Superintendent of Documents Classification Number Index to the Cumulative Subject Guide to U.S. Government Bibliographies, 1924–1973* (1977).

General Catalogs and Indexes

New and comprehensive indexes to federal documents, especially congressional documents, are discussed below, but they do not obviate the need to use older well-known catalogs and indexes. These old volumes are overlapping and some are incomplete; all take a little hands-on experience before they easily yield up their treasures. But time spent in getting acquainted is well worthwhile, for different perspectives and modes of indexing are especially important in searching for government documents.

The earliest attempt to provide a comprehensive guide to published documents, from all branches of the federal government, is [563] *A Descriptive Catalogue of the Government Publications of the United States, September 5, 1774–March 4, 1881*, by Ben Perley Poore (Washington: Government Printing Office, 1885; also issued as *Senate Miscellaneous Document* no. 67, 48th Congress, 2d session, serial 2268). This work contains 1,241 pages of catalog, in which the entries are arranged chronologically, and 148 pages of index. There is a considerable amount of confusion in citations, and the lists are incomplete. The work also takes some practice to use. The index refers only to pages, and one must then run a finger down two columns of material to locate the pertinent item. Most of the items are congressional documents, but the *Catalogue* does not indicate the serial number of the volume in which the document appears; that number must be looked up in the *Checklist* [565]. Yet there is a wealth of material to be located by means of Poore's *Catalogue,* and patience pays off.

Poore's volume is followed by [564] *Comprehensive Index to the Publications of the United States Government, 1881–1893*, by John G. Ames, 2 vols. (Washington: Government Printing Office, 1905; issued as *House Document* no. 754, 58th Congress, 2d session, serials 4745–

4746). Documents are listed under subject entries. Although called "comprehensive," the work is not absolutely complete.

A most useful volume is [565] *Checklist of United States Public Documents, 1789–1909: Congressional, to Close of Sixtieth Congress; Departmental, to End of the Calendar Year 1909*, 3d rev. and enl. ed. (Washington: Government Printing Office, 1911). This stocky volume of 1,707 pages is not a dictionary catalog but instead arranges material by issuing agencies. It is in essence a shelflist for documents in the library of the Superintendent of Documents and provides the superintendent's classification numbers (called SuDoc numbers) for the various classes of documents. Since many libraries today identify and shelve public documents under this classification scheme, the *Checklist* is a handy guide to the materials within its chronological coverage. The volume also contains tables indicating the congressional documents in each volume of the Congressional Serial Set [597].

Now there is a new guide to documents in the *Checklist*: [566] *CIS Index to US Executive Branch Documents, 1789–1909: Guide to Documents Listed in Checklist of US Public Documents, 1789–1909, Not Printed in the U.S. Serial Set*, 6 parts (Bethesda, Md.: Congressional Information Service, 1990—), which has an announced completion date of 1995. It provides multiple types of access, and there is an accompanying microfiche collection of all the documents indexed. Arranged by government department or agency, the *Index* has five sections: a reference bibliography that provides full bibliographic data for each document, and indexes by subjects and names, Superintendent of Documents numbers, agency report numbers, and titles. As the subtitle notes, however, this publication (and the microfiche) omit documents listed in the *Checklist* that appear in the Congressional Serial Set (and some other classes of material). The Congressional Information Service (CIS) intends to extend the chronological coverage of this publication, with documents from 1910 to the early 1920s starting in 1994 and additional time periods to follow.

Ames's *Comprehensive Index* is followed in sequence by [567] *Catalogue of the Public Documents of the . . . Congress and of All Departments of the Government of the United States*, 25 vols. (Washington: Government Printing Office, 1896–1945). This series, often called simply the *Document Catalog*, runs from the 53d Congress (1893–1895) through the 76th Congress (1939–1941), generally with a volume for each congress.

Because Congress failed to authorize continuation of the *Document Catalog* beyond 1941, reliance must be placed after that date on the [568] *Monthly Catalog of United States Government Publications* (Washington: Government Printing Office, 1895–), which began publication in January 1895. The arrangement is primarily alphabetical by issuing office. Indexes appear monthly and annually, and there are 5- and 10-year cumulative indexes. These indexes can be supplemented by a series of author indexes to the *Monthly Catalog*: [569] *Decennial Cumulative Personal Author Index, 1941–1950*, by Edward Przebienda (Ann Arbor, Mich.: Pierian Press, 1971); *1951–1960* (1971); *Quinquennial, 1961–1965*; and *1966–1970* (1972). A commercial publisher has issued comprehensive indexes: [570] *Cumulative Subject Index to the Monthly Catalog of United States Government Publications, 1900–1971*, compiled by William W. Buchanan and Edna M. Kanely, 15 vols. (Washington: Carrollton Press, 1973–1975), and [571] *Cumulative Subject Index to the Monthly Catalog of United States Government Publications, 1895–1899*, by Edna A. Kanely, 2 vols. (Washington: Carrollton Press, 1977). The *Monthly Catalog* is helpful for keeping in touch with government publications on a current basis, and it is often the last resort for researchers seeking historical documents from the twentieth century. From 1976 on the *Monthly Catalog* has been available online as [572] *GPO Monthly Catalog* from a variety of vendors; and, under varying titles, it is available on CD-ROMs for the same time period. The online and CD-ROM versions are periodically updated.

An author index representing pre-1956 holdings in American libraries reported to the National Union Catalog in the Library of Congress is [573] *United States Government Publications*, 16 vols. (London: Mansell, 1980). This is a reprinting of volumes 609–624 of *The National Union Catalog, Pre-1956 Imprints* [21], and only the first volume bears the new title. The other volumes carry the original title pages.

An extensive collection of printed public documents exists in the Public Documents Library of the Government Printing Office, which is now in National Archives Record Group 287. The [574] *Cumulative Title Index to United States Public Documents, 1789–1976*, compiled by Daniel W. Lester, Sandra K. Faull, and Lorraine E. Lester, 16 vols. (Arlington, Va.: United States Historical Documents Institute, 1979–1982), can be helpful in tracking down or verifying items.

A valuable annual index is [575] *Guide to U.S. Government Publications*, by Donna Andriot (McLean, Va.: Documents Index, 1991–);

earlier editions, edited by John L. Andriot, were published beginning in 1959, at first under the title *Guide to U.S. Government Serials and Periodicals*. This work lists publications by issuing agency (including the classification number of the Superintendent of Documents), with reference to classes of documents, not to individual documents. Agency and title indexes are provided. This guide is a handy reference for locating the classification number for documents in libraries using the Superintendent of Documents system. The *Guide* includes an essay, "A Practical Guide to the Superintendent of Documents Classification System," which supplies an extended introduction to the numbering system.

Congressional Publications

Access to congressional documents has been revolutionized by the exhaustive and accurate publications of the Congressional Information Service, which provide information about current publications of Congress as well as retrospective indexes. Beginning in 1970, there is a monthly [576] *CIS/Index,* cumulated each year in a [577] *CIS/Annual.* At the start there were two parts to each *Annual*: Part One, *Abstracts,* furnishes information about congressional publications, arranged by House and Senate committees or other groups within Congress. Each abstract supplies bibliographical information about a document, including Superintendent of Documents classification number, as well as a brief outline of its contents. Through 1983 the *Abstracts* volume also included brief legislative histories for the laws passed during the year. Part Two, *Index,* supplies an alphabetical subject and names index, as well as supplementary indexes (by titles, bill numbers, report and document numbers, hearings numbers, and Superintendent of Documents numbers). There are cumulative subject indexes for 1970–1974, 1975–1978, and 1979–1982. Beginning in 1984, a Part Three, *Legislative Histories of US Public Laws,* has been included. For each significant public law, *Legislative Histories* provides an abstract of the law with full bibliographical citation and notes the course of legislation through slip laws, committee reports, the *Congressional Record,* committee hearings, committee prints, House and Senate documents, and the *Weekly Compilation of Presidential Documents* [644]. There are indexes to subjects and names, titles, and bill numbers.

   In addition to the abstracts and indexes the firm publishes the [578] *CIS/Microfiche Library,* which provides in microfiche most of the items listed in its indexes.

The Congressional Information Service's massive retrospective indexes for the Congressional Serial Set, Committee Hearings, Committee Prints, and other classes of documents will be described in appropriate places below.

Although the CIS retrospective indexes largely supersede older catalogs and indexes to congressional materials, some of the old items may still be useful for supplementary searches. To the catalogs listed in the section "General Catalogs and Indexes" above can be added the following:

[579] *Public Documents of the First Fourteen Congresses, 1789–1817: Papers Relating to Early Congressional Documents,* by A. W. Greely (Washington: Government Printing Office, 1900; issued as *Senate Document* no. 428, 56th Congress, 1st session, serial 3879). A supplement, "Public Documents of the First Fourteen Congresses," appeared in *Annual Report of the American Historical Association for the Year 1903,* 1: 343–406, and was issued also as *House Document* no. 745, 58th Congress, 2d session, serial 4735. These are chronological catalogs.

[580] *Tables of and Annotated Index to the Congressional Series of United States Public Documents* (Washington: Government Printing Office, 1902). This is a selected list of congressional documents from the 15th to the 52d Congress (1817–1893) and parallels material printed in Poore's *Descriptive Catalogue* [563] and Ames's *Comprehensive Index* [564], but it often helps to approach the material through more than one index.

In order to obtain serial numbers for congressional reports and documents, which since 1941 have been listed in the *Monthly Catalog* without serial numbers, it is necessary to use the series [581] *Numerical Lists and Schedule of Volumes of the Reports and Documents of . . . Congress* (Washington: Government Printing Office, 1934–1982). The *Numerical Lists,* however, stopped publication with the 96th Congress (1980) and volume 13,384 of the Congressional Serial Set. For the 97th Congress (1981–1982) serial numbers can be located in [582] *United States Congressional Serial Set Supplement* to the *Monthly Catalog,* published by the Superintendent of Documents in 1985. It lists the documents in the order in which they appear in the Congressional Serial Set and provides serial numbers; there are a variety of indexes to the documents. Review and evaluation by the Congressional Serial Set Committee, however, led to a new publication beginning with the 98th Congress (1983–1984): [583]

United States Congressional Serial Set Catalog: Numerical Lists and Schedules of Volumes, which appears biennially. It follows the format of the *Numerical Lists* but includes detailed author, title, subject, series, and bill number indexes.

Congressional Proceedings

The official journals of Congress record in brief form the action taken on legislation. They are the simplest way to follow the full legislative history of bills introduced in Congress. The original journals for the early congresses are difficult to locate, but there are reprintings of them, as follows:

[584] *Journal of the Senate,* 5 vols. (Washington: Gales and Seaton, 1820–1821). The first thirteen congresses (1789–1815).

[585] *Journal of the House of Representatives,* 9 vols. (Washington: Gales and Seaton, 1826). The first thirteen congresses (1789–1815).

[586] *Congressional Journals of the United States,* 1789–1817, 65 vols. (Wilmington, Del.: Michael Glazier, 1977). There are eight series, one for the House and another for the Senate for each of the first four presidents.

An excellent new edition of early congressional journals is [587] *Documentary History of the First Federal Congress of the United States of America,* vols. 1–3, edited by Linda Grant De Pauw (Baltimore: Johns Hopkins University Press, 1972–1977), which contains the Senate legislative journal, the Senate executive journal and related documents, and the House of Representatives journal for that congress.

From the 15th Congress (1817) to the 82d Congress (1954), the *House Journal* and the *Senate Journal* for each session appear in the Congressional Serial Set [597]. Each volume is indexed separately by both subject matter and bill number. There are general indexes to the journals of the first sixteen congresses only, prepared by Albert Ordway.

When the Senate is in executive session to consider treaties or to confirm appointments of government officials, the proceedings are not contained in the regular journals. From time to time, however, the Senate has authorized the publication of these special proceedings as [588] *Journal of the Executive Proceedings of the Senate of the United States,* vols. 1–3 (Washington: Duff Green, 1828); vols. 4– (Washington: Government Printing Office, 1887–). The series has been reprinted through the 59th Congress (1905–1906) by Johnson Reprint Corporation, 1969.

In print, also, are [589] *Journals of the Continental Congress,* 1774–

1789, edited by Worthington Chauncey Ford and others, 34 vols. (Washington: Government Printing Office, 1904–1937). This comprehensive publication supersedes the contemporary printings and early reprints. The journals include a great many reports and other documents as well as the strict account of official proceedings. There is a cumulative index: *Index, Journals of the Continental Congress, 1774–1789* [689].

Congressional Debates

The reports of actual debates in Congress appear in four series. In the beginning the reports were not verbatim but were in the nature of abstracts, gathered together at first from newspapers of the day and other sources and were written in the third person. Sometime in the 1850s the debates began to appear in the first person and approached a verbatim report. An interesting account of the material in the various series of debates is given in *Government Publications and Their Use* [557], pp. 134–44.

The first series is generally known as [590] *Annals of Congress* (full title: *The Debates and Proceedings in the Congress of the United States; with an Appendix, Containing Important State Papers and Public Documents and All the Laws of a Public Nature; with a Copious Index*). It comprises 42 volumes and covers the first seventeen congresses and the first session of the 18th Congress (1789–1824). The volumes were not contemporaneous publications but were issued from 1834 to 1856 by Gales and Seaton, a commercial printer. A modern compilation of debates for the 1st Congress (1789–1791), is [591] *Documentary History of the First Federal Congress of the United States of America,* vols 10, 11, and others in progress, *Debates in the House of Representatives,* edited by Charlene Bangs Bickford, Kenneth R. Bowling, and Helen E. Veit (Baltimore: Johns Hopkins University Press, 1992–). The five volumes planned for House of Representatives debates will replace the *Annals* for that period and will contain more than twice as much material as the *Annals,* drawn from a variety of sources including a transcription of shorthand notes taken by Thomas Lloyd on the floor of the House.

The second series is [592] *Register of Debates in Congress,* 14 volumes, published by Gales and Seaton from 1825 to 1837; it covers the second session of the 18th Congress through the first session of the 25th Congress (1824–1837). These volumes were issued contemporaneously with the proceedings but are not a verbatim record of the debates.

The third series, which overlaps the preceding series, is [593] *The Congressional Globe*. It comprises 109 books in 46 volumes, from the first session of the 23d Congress through the 42d Congress (1833–1873). There is some confusion about the numbering of the volumes, and it is therefore better to cite the *Globe* by congress and session rather than by volume number. Like its predecessors, the *Globe* was published by a commercial printer.

These series of debates have indexes in the separate volumes for proceedings in the House and in the Senate. Some of the volumes also contain appendixes, which should be searched for pertinent material. The sessions and dates covered by the separate volumes can be found in the *Checklist of United States Public Documents* [565], pp. 1463–75.

The [594] *Congressional Record* began publication with the first session of the 43d Congress in 1873 and has appeared continuously ever since. It is printed by the Government Printing Office. It appears to be a complete and verbatim report of debates, but neither the daily *Record* (printed for the use of Congress) nor the permanently bound *Record* is exactly that. Material from the daily edition can be edited before it appears in the permanent edition, and a good many speeches and other materials were never actually uttered on the floor of Congress but were inserted under a leave-to-print privilege. Indexes have been prepared for each session of Congress for the bound volumes. The *Congressional Record* in full text from 1985 to the present, produced by the Superintendent of Documents, is available online through such services as LEXIS, NEXIS, and WESTLAW and is updated daily.

Documents and Reports

Items ordered to be printed by the Senate or House are considered congressional documents. They include reports of congressional committees, reports of special investigations, and memorials submitted to Congress, for example. The documents cover a wide variety of topics and are a rich resource for researchers in United States history, for there is material on social, scientific, economic, and other nonpolitical aspects of the nation's past, some of it not government related at all. They also include extensive material originating in the executive branch of the government, such as messages of the president to Congress, annual reports of the cabinet members (often including the reports of their subordinates), and reports on a great variety of topics submitted in response to resolutions of the House or Senate.

Congressional documents are organized according to the sessions of Congress. Each congress, which runs for two years, is divided into a number of distinct sessions—ordinarily two, but in some congresses three, with occasionally a special session. (A convenient place to learn the inclusive dates of each session is the *Biographical Directory of the American Congress* [612].) The official designation of the various items has changed through the years; common classifications since the 15th Congress are House Reports, House Documents, House Executive Documents, and House Miscellaneous Documents, with a similar set of classifications for the Senate. Items in these categories are numbered serially by session or in later years only by congress. Since many of the reports originate in congressional committees, it might be convenient at times to use [595] *Congressional Committees, 1789–1982: A Checklist,* by Walter Stubbs (Westport, Conn.: Greenwood Press, 1985), which lists 1,516 committees and provides data on their establishment and termination.

Documents from the early national period appear in [596] *American State Papers: Documents Legislative and Executive of the Congress of the United States,* 38 vols. (Washington: Gales and Seaton, 1832–1861). The volumes are arranged in ten classes, as follows:

1. *Foreign Relations,* 6 vols., June 11, 1789, to May 24, 1828.
2. *Indian Affairs,* 2 vols., May 25, 1789, to March 1, 1827.
3. *Finance,* 5 vols., April 11, 1789, to May 16, 1828.
4. *Commerce and Navigation,* 2 vols., April 13, 1789, to February 25, 1823.
5. *Military Affairs,* 7 vols., August 10, 1879, to March 1, 1838.
6. *Naval Affairs,* 4 vols., January 20, 1794, to June 15, 1836.
7. *Post Office Department,* 1 vol., January 22, 1790, to February 1, 1833.
8. *Public Lands,* 8 vols., July 31, 1789, to February 28, 1837.
9. *Claims,* 1 vol., February 5, 1790, to March 3, 1823.
10. *Miscellaneous,* 2 vols., April 18, 1789, to March 3, 1823.

Most of the congressional documents are printed in a massive set of volumes usually called the [597] Congressional Serial Set. The series begins with the 15th Congress (1817), and the volumes are shelved by serial numbers, assigned consecutively to volumes of documents produced by each session of Congress. As of December 1992 there were approximately 14,000 volumes in the Serial Set. The serial number of the volume in which a particular document is published is usually the quickest way to find the document in a library.

The chief retrospective index to the Serial Set is now the [598] *CIS US Serial Set Index,* 36 vols. (Washington: Congressional Information

Service, 1975–1979). It is published in twelve consecutive parts, each covering a given sequence of congresses. As a whole it runs from 1789 through 1969, thus covering the years up to the beginning of the *CIS/Annual* [577]. For each part there is an Index of Subjects and Keywords, a Numerical List of Reports and Documents, a Schedule of Serial Volumes, and an Index of Names of Individuals and Organizations cited in private relief bills and related actions. The *Index* also covers the *American State Papers* [596], which in some libraries has been assigned serial numbers 01–038. The *Index* is a godsend for researchers. The numerical lists give a document-by-document listing, with an indication of the serial number of the volumes in which they are contained. One can often find pertinent documents for a particular year or span of years by running down these lists. The subject indexes are detailed and useful, even though they are compiled in general from the titles of the documents, and thus comparable documents might appear under a variety of titles. Access is possible online and through CD-ROM in *Congressional Masterfile 1* [608].

Although most researchers will find what they need in the *CIS US Serial Set Index,* the catalogs listed above in the section "General Catalogs and Indexes" may still be of use, for they offer alternative indexing to Serial Set documents for the years they cover. There are also some old indexes to congressional documents and reports, cited in *Government Publications and Their Use* [557], pp. 31–32. An index on one subject is [599] *Guide to American Indian Documents in the Congressional Serial Set, 1817–1899,* by Steven L. Johnson (New York: Clearwater Publishing Company, 1977).

A recent reference work on special Senate documents is [599A] *CIS Index to US Senate Executive Documents and Reports, Covering Documents and Reports Not Printed in the US Serial Set, 1817–1969,* 2 vols. (Washington: Congressional Information Service, 1987). The work lists documents (usually confidential at the time they were produced) printed for the use of the senators when considering treaties and presidential nominations in executive session. The bulk of the material deals with treaties, including those with American Indians, and the index pulls together documents from scattered repositories. Although many of these documents in original manuscript form are in the Senate treaty ratification files in the National Archives, this index makes possible easy use of materials regarding ratification of treaties that otherwise would be difficult to locate and use. The introduction to the index describes the nature and scope of the documents. Complete texts of the documents them-selves are available on accompanying CIS microfiche.

Bills and Resolutions

To trace legislation completely, it is often necessary to consult the var-ious bills introduced in their original form and in their various amended versions short of the final law. Bills and resolutions (and their amend-ments) in printed form are issued for use of members of Congress. They are numbered in series, beginning with each congress. The printed bills are not readily available, especially for early congresses. The Library of Congress has an extensive set, which has been microfilmed and thus made more widely available. The microfilm set, issued by the Library of Congress Photoduplication Service (1931–1933), covers the lst Congress through the 72d Congress. The Congressional Information Service is-sues [600] *CIS Congressional Bills, Resolutions, and Laws on Micro-fiche* for each congress from the 73d Congress (1933–1934) to the pre-sent. The United States Superintendent of Documents now issues the bills and resolutions on microfiche and publishes an annual [601] *Cu-mulative Finding Aid, House and Senate Bills (Microfiche Format)*. The bills and resolutions can be consulted also in the Office of the Clerk of the House of Representatives, the Office of the Secretary of the Senate, and the National Archives.

Committee Hearings

Important material is found in transcripts of hearings before House and Senate committees. The hearings consider legislation, deal with over-sight of government operations, or review matters of public concern. Witnesses are called from many walks of life, and frequently they pre-pare extensive presentations, which may be summarized orally and then the written form inserted into the printed transcripts. The data offered in the testimony at the hearings are extensive and often very valuable. A few hearings appear as documents or reports published in the Congres-sional Serial Set, but most of them, especially in recent decades, have been printed outside the regular series of congressional documents. They are identified by the name of the committee, the session of Congress, and the number of the bill on which the hearings are held. The hearings have titles, which are necessary for locating the documents in some library catalogs.

As they are published, hearings are listed in the *Monthly Catalog* and in the *CIS/Index*. The best retrospective index to the hearings is [602] *CIS US Congressional Committee Hearings Index,* 42 vols. (Washington: Congressional Information Service, 1981–1985). This series covers the 23d Congress (1833) through the 91st Congress (1969), after which the hearings can be located in the *CIS/Annual*. The series is published in eight parts, each with five or six volumes and covering a set span of years. Each part includes a reference bibliography with bibliographic data, subject descriptors, and witness names for each document; an index of subjects and organizations; an index by personal names, including both persons who testify and those who are subjects of testimony; and supplementary indexes for titles, bill numbers, Superintendent of Documents classification numbers, and numbers for related reports and documents. The data are included in *Congressional Masterfile 1* [608]. The Congressional Information Service has published the whole series of hearings on microfiche.

A good many hearings are not included in the published series of hearings but exist only as transcripts, which have now been compiled and issued on microfiche. They can be located in the following indexes:

[603] *CIS Index to Unpublished US Senate Committee Hearings, 18th Congress—88th Congress, 1823–1964,* 5 vols. (Bethesda, Md.: Congressional Information Service, 1986).

[604] *CIS Index to Unpublished US Senate Committee Hearings, 89th Congress—90th Congress, 1965–1968* (Bethesda, Md.: Congressional Information Service, 1989).

[605] *CIS Index to Unpublished US House of Representatives Committee Hearings, 1833–1936,* 2 vols. (Bethesda, Md.: Congressional Information Service, 1988).

[606] *CIS Index to Unpublished US House of Representatives Committee Hearings, 1937–1946,* 2 vols. (Bethesda, Md.: Congressional Information Service, 1990).

These indexes all provide a reference bibliography and indexes by subjects and organizations, personal names, titles, and bill numbers.

There are some older printed indexes to congressional committee hearings, whose titles are given in *Government Publications and Their Use* [557], pp. 180–83, but they have been largely superseded by the *CIS US Congressional Committee Hearings Index* [602].

Committee Prints

Congressional committees, especially in recent decades, have directed the printing of material that is useful to them in their deliberations. The reports and other data are provided by professional staff members of the committees, by outside consultants, or by the Congressional Research Service of the Library of Congress. At times existing publications are reprinted. The resultant publications are called committee prints; they provide much information, often otherwise difficult to find, relating to the various committees' responsibilities.

The best access to current committee prints is through the *CIS/Index* and the *CIS/Annual*. Retrospectively, the committee prints are indexed in [607] *CIS US Congressional Committee Prints Index: From the Earliest Publications through 1969*, 5 vols. (Washington: Congressional Information Service, 1980). This index gives bibliographic data and annotations for all publications, an index by subjects and names, and finding aids such as index by titles, index by congress and committee, index by bill numbers, and index by Superintendent of Documents number. The *Index* is accessible online and on CD-ROM in *Congressional Masterfile 1* [608].

CIS Indexes on CD-ROM

The indexes to congressional documents published by the Congressional Information Service, both retrospective and current ones, are available in machine-readable form on CD-ROMs:

[608] *Congressional Masterfile 1* incorporates the detailed indexing of the following retrospective indexes: *CIS US Serial Set Index* [598], *CIS Congressional Hearings Index* [602], *CIS US Congressional Committee Prints Index* [607], *CIS Index to US Senate Executive Documents and Reports* [566], *CIS Index to Unpublished US Senate Committee Hearings* [603–604], and *CIS Index to Unpublished US House of Representatives Committee Hearings* [605–606].

[609] *Congressional Masterfile 2* incorporates the indexing of *CIS/Index* [576] and *CIS/Annual* [577] from 1970 to the present. A retrospective disc covers 1970–1988, and a current disc, updated quarterly, covers 1989 on. These include legislative histories.

Other Guides

Congressional documents in the National Archives are described in *Guide to the Records of the United States House of Representatives at the National Archives, 1789–1989* [684], and *Guide to the Records of the United States Senate at the National Archives, 1789–1989* [685].

For each congress there is the [610] *Congressional Directory* (also called the *Official Congressional Directory*), which began publication in 1809 and for the early years was issued by private firms. It provides biographical data on the members of Congress and other information about Congress and about other branches of the government as well. A compilation of early directories is [611] *The United States Congressional Directories, 1789–1840*, edited by Perry M. Goldman and James S. Young (New York: Columbia University Press, 1973).

An extremely useful reference work is [612] *Biographical Directory of the American Congress, 1774–1989*, Bicentennial Edition (Washington: Government Printing Office, 1989; issued as *Senate Document* no. 100–34, 100th Congress, 2d session), which completely revises and updates previous editions. It provides a roster of all members for each congress and a brief biographical sketch of all persons who have served in Congress, including those in the Continental Congress, and it notes available bibliographical references.

The papers of members of the House of Representatives and of the Senate have not been systematically collected, and Congress has made no provision for the preservation of the papers (as it has done for those of the presidents of the United States). Papers appear in the Library of Congress and in a great many other repositories. They can be located through the guides to manuscript collections discussed in chapter 8. Of special value are the recent [613] *Guide to Research Collections of Former United States Senators, 1789–1982*, by Kathryn Allamong Jacob and Elizabeth Ann Hornyak (Washington: Historical Office, United States Senate, 1983), and [614] *A Guide to Research Collections of Former Members of the United States House of Representatives, 1789–1987*, by Raymond W. Smock and Cynthia Pease Miller (Washington: United States House of Representatives, 1988). These volumes, prepared as bicentennial publications, provide access to research materials for 3,300 members of the House and 1,800 senators found in repositories throughout the United States. See also [615] *Members of Congress: A Checklist of Their Papers in the Manuscript Division, Library of Congress*, by John J. McDonough (Washington: Library of Congress, 1980), and [616]

The Speakers of the U.S. House of Representatives: A Bibliography, 1789–1984, by Donald R. Kennon (Baltimore: Johns Hopkins University Press, 1985).

Federal Laws and Treaties

The end product of the legislative process, with its debates, reports, and hearings, is a federal law, once the president has approved the action of Congress. The published laws are an important source of information for historians, and the legislative history of individual public laws is often significant. An exhaustive and well-edited collection of documents detailing the course of legislation in the 1st Congress is [617] *Documentary History of the First Federal Congress of the United States of America*, vols. 4–6, *Legislative Histories*, edited by Charlene Bangs Bickford and Helen E. Veit (Baltimore: Johns Hopkins University Press, 1986). Other legislative histories can be found in [618] *Sources of Compiled Legislative Histories: A Bibliography of Government Documents, Periodical Articles, and Books, 1st Congress–94th Congress*, by Nancy P. Johnson (Littleton, Colo.: Fred B. Rothman, for the American Association of Law Libraries, 1979), and [619] *Legislative Reference Checklist: The Key to Legislative Histories from 1789–1903*, by Eugene Nabors (Littleton, Colo.: Fred B. Rothman, 1982), which furnishes bill numbers for laws and resolutions. See also *CIS/Annual*, Part Three, *Legislative Histories of US Public Laws* [577].

Statutes at Large

Federal laws are published in permanent form in [620] *Statutes at Large of the United States*, a continuing series from 1789 to the present, which contains both public and private acts. The laws are printed in chronological order. Volume 5 has an index for the five volumes; volume 8, one for the first eight. Later volumes have separate indexes.

There are a number of composite or extended indexes to the *Statutes at Large*. For a description of them, see *Government Publications and Their Use* [557], pp. 221–26.

Codifications

The *Statutes at Large* are generally the series of laws that historians use, for they show developing legislation in a chronological order. These laws, however, from time to time have been codified, that is, the laws in force at a given time have been systematized and printed. The first codification was the [621] *Revised Statutes,* enacted on June 27, 1874, and comprising the permanent law in force on December 1, 1873. It appeared as part 1 of volume 18 of the *Statutes at Large.* A corrected edition was issued in 1878 as [622] *Second Edition, Revised Statutes of the United States Passed at the 1st Session of the 43d Congress.* Two supplements were issued, one covering laws of the 43d to the 51st Congresses (1874–1891) and the other, laws of the 52d to the 56th Congresses (1892–1901).

A new codification was approved on June 30, 1926, of permanent laws in force on December 7, 1925. It has a detailed title but is generally known as the [623] *United States Code*; it is published by the United States Government Printing Office. New editions have been issued from time to time; the current *Code* appeared in 1988 in 28 volumes, of which seven are a general index, and there have been annual supplements. The *Code* is divided into fifty titles, each devoted to a particular field or subject; thus Title 10 deals with the Armed Forces, Title 25 with Indians, Title 39 with the Postal Service, and so on.

Occasionally compilations of laws pertaining to specific subjects have been published. Some of these are discussed in *Government Publications and Their Use* [557], pp. 226–55.

Treaties

Up to 1950, treaties were printed in the *Statutes at Large.* Volume 7 comprised Indian treaties up to that date and volume 8 treaties with foreign nations. Subsequently treaties were included in later volumes of the *Statutes.* A number of compilations of treaties are valuable for historical research, not only for texts of the treaties but for annotations and related documents. The following are the standard ones.

[624] *Treaties, Conventions, International Acts, Protocols, and Agreements between the United States of America and Other Powers,* by William M. Malloy, 2 vols. (Washington: Government Printing Office, 1910). Malloy's volumes cover 1776–1909. Two other volumes were published: vol. 3, edited by C. F. Richard (covering 1910–1923), and vol. 4, edited by Edward J. Trenwith (covering 1923–1937).

[625] *Treaties and Other International Acts of the United States of America,* edited by Hunter Miller, 8 vols. (Washington: Government

Printing Office, 1931–1948). This work, valuable for its extensive annotations, carries the treaties only to 1863.

[626] *Treaties and Other International Agreements of the United States of America, 1776–1949,* edited by Charles I. Bevens, 12 vols. (Washington: United States Department of State, 1968–1974). A *General Index* was published as vol. 13 in 1976.

[627] *Treaties and Other International Agreements of the United States of America* (Washington: Government Printing Office, 1952–). This continuing series, beginning with the year 1950, is the official publication of treaties and replaces publication in the *Statutes at Large.*

See also [628] *Unperfected Treaties of the United States of America, 1776–1976,* 6 vols. to date (Dobbs Ferry, N.Y.: Oceana Publications, 1976–). Vol. 6 (1984) carries the series to 1925.

A comprehensive index is [629] *United States Treaty Index: 1776–1990 Consolidation,* by Igor I. Kavass, 11 vols. (Buffalo, N.Y.: William S. Hein and Company, 1991), which is divided into a *Master Guide* (in numerical order), 5 vols.; *Chronological Index,* 2 vols.; *Country Index,* 2 vols.; and *Subject Index,* 2 vols. This publication replaces previous treaty indexes compiled by Igor I. Kavass and others, published by Hein. It is available in machine-readable form as [630] *Hein's United States Treaty Index on CD-ROM,* which is updated periodically. See also [631] *A Guide to the United States Treaties in Force,* by Igor I. Kavass and Adolf Sprudzs, 2 parts (Buffalo, N.Y.: William S. Hein and Company, 1983).

Treaties with American Indian tribes do not appear in the compilations of treaties listed above. They were published in the *Statutes at Large,* vol. 7 and later volumes. The standard compilation of these treaties is [632] *Indian Affairs: Laws and Treaties,* vol. 2, *Treaties,* compiled by Charles J. Kappler (Washington: Government Printing Office, 1904).

Records of the Executive Branch

Many executive records, such as presidential messages to Congress, annual reports of cabinet departments and subordinate agencies, and special reports compiled at the request of the House or the Senate, are printed in the Congressional Serial Set [597] and can be located in the *CIS US Serial Set Index* [598]. Other departmental and agency records are listed in the general catalogs to government documents cited above.

Of special usefulness is *CIS Index to US Executive Branch Documents, 1789–1909* [566].

Administrative Regulations and Rulings

Congress has conferred considerable power upon agencies of the executive branch for the conduct of business, and administrative regulations and rulings almost rival the legislation of Congress in importance. A law of July 26, 1935, directed the publication of regulations of the executive agencies in the [633] *Federal Register,* which was first issued on March 14, 1936. It has become a mammoth publication, running to tens of thousands of pages each year. It appears daily on work days, and a series of bound volumes is issued for each year (with continuous pagination). Indexes are issued monthly, quarterly, and annually. A widely used index is [634] *CIS Federal Register Index* (Bethesda, Md.: Congressional Information Service, 1984–). It appears weekly with interim paperbound cumulations issued approximately every 5 weeks. These paperbound issues are replaced by permanent semiannual cumulations. These are indexes by subjects and names, *CFR* section numbers, and federal agency docket numbers. The *Federal Register* for recent years is available in full text online from a number of services and on CD-ROM.

Permanent regulations are codified in the [635] *Code of Federal Regulations (CFR),* which is divided into titles, generally corresponding to those in the *United States Code,* with a separate volume or volumes for each title. The *CFR* is revised annually. A current annual index is [636] *Index to the Code of Federal Regulations 1991: Subject Index,* 4 vols. (Bethesda, Md.: Congressional Information Service, 1992), which updates earlier editions covering 1977–1990. It will be updated by *Index Supplements.*

Departmental rulings and opinions of legal officers have been published in large numbers. Examples are *Official Opinions of the Attorneys General, Digest of Opinions of the Judge Advocate General of the Army, Opinions and Decisions of the Atomic Energy Commission, Decisions of the Comptroller of the Treasury, Federal Trade Commission Decisions,* and *Decisions of the Interstate Commerce Commission.* There is a discussion of such publications in *Government Publications and Their Use* [557], pp. 304–29.

Foreign Affairs

The conduct of foreign affairs is largely an executive function (with the advice and consent of the Senate), and students of diplomatic history must rely heavily on documents generated by the executive branch. A guide to early publications is [637] *Index to United States Documents Relating to Foreign Affairs, 1828–1861*, by Adelaide R. Hasse, 3 vols. (Washington: Carnegie Institution, 1914–1921). The Department of State has published a continuing series of volumes (with documents from 1861 on), now called [638] *Foreign Relations of the United States* (Washington: Government Printing Office, 1862–), which, despite continued agitation from historians and others, is far behind in publication. See also *A Reference Guide to United States Department of State Special Files* [686], and *Select Catalog of National Archives Microfilm Publications: Diplomatic Records* [696].

A new publication that indexes and furnishes abstracts of key nonclassified federal documents that deal with foreign affairs, beginning in 1993, is [639] *American Foreign Policy Index* (Bethesda, Md.: Congressional Information Service, 1993–), issued quarterly with annual cumulations. There is a microfiche collection of the documents in full text.

A modern, up-to-date reference work on diplomatic history is *Guide to American Foreign Relations since 1700* [138]. This *Guide* supersedes the [640] *Guide to the Diplomatic History of the United States, 1775– 1921*, by Samuel Flagg Bemis and Grace Gardner Griffin (Washington: Government Printing Office, 1935), which for many years was the standard reference work. A general introductory guide is [641] *U.S. Foreign Relations: A Guide to Information Sources,* by Elmer Plischke (Detroit: Gale Research Company, 1980).

Presidential Papers

An early and still very useful compilation of presidential documents is [642] *A Compilation of the Messages and Papers of the Presidents, 1789–1897*, compiled by James D. Richardson, 10 vols. (Washington: Government Printing Office, 1896–1899; also issued as *House Miscellaneous Document* no. 210, 53d Congress, 2d session, serial 3265, parts 1– 10). This is a selective compilation, but much of value is to be found in it. The original Richardson volumes carried the documents into President McKinley's term, and a supplement issued in 1903 carried the documents to August 1902. There followed a number of commercial sets that incorporated the official volumes and extended their coverage. Some of them adopted continuous pagination, and a researcher must be careful to cite exact publication data to match the pagination used. Ultimately these sets carried the documents into Coolidge's administration. A guide through this publication maze is provided in *Government Publications and Their Use* [557], pp. 331–35.

Much more complete is the series entitled [643] *Public Papers of the Presidents of the United States,* published by the Government Printing Office, a multivolume series for each president beginning with Harry S. Truman (papers for Herbert Hoover have been published also). The basic text consists of speeches or comments made by the president and written documents signed by him. From 1965 on, presidential documents have been printed in the [644] *Weekly Compilation of Presidential Documents.* This publication is now paginated continuously so that the issues can be used to form the *Public Papers.* Kraus International Publishers has issued a number of [645] *Cumulated Indexes to the Public Papers of the Presidents of the United States,* which combine the separate indexes in the volumes for a given president into one alphabetical index.

Executive orders of the president are listed in the *Monthly Catalog* [568], are printed in the *Federal Register* [633], and appear in Title 3 of the *Code of Federal Regulations* [635]. A list and index to earlier executive orders is [646] *Presidential Executive Orders,* compiled by the WPA Historical Records Survey and edited by Clifford L. Lord (New York: Archives Publishing Company, 1944), which lists orders numbered 1 to 8,030, issued 1862–1938. A more recent and comprehensive guide is [647] *CIS Index to Presidential Executive Orders and Proclamations,* 22 vols., including a 2-vol. *Supplement* (Bethesda, Md.: Congressional Information Service, 1987). It provides access to some 75,000 documents issued from 1789 to 1983, which include both numbered and unnumbered orders and also proclamations. There is a collection of microfiche that contains the full text of all the documents. After 1983, executive orders and proclamations can be located by use of the *Index to the Code of Federal Regulations* [636].

A useful compilation of presidential material, especially because of the detailed index, is [648] *The State of the Union Messages of the Presidents, 1790–1966,* edited by Fred L. Israel, 3 vols. (New York: Chelsea House, 1966).

Manuscript papers of the presidents in the Library of Congress and indexes to them are noted above [374]; for presidents beginning with

Franklin Delano Roosevelt, the presidential libraries that are part of the National Archives contain extensive files of documents (see the section on Presidential Libraries in chapter 14 and *Guide to Manuscripts in the Presidential Libraries* [694]). General reference works that deal with research materials on the presidents are [649] *Presidential Libraries and Collections,* by Fritz Veit (Westport, Conn.: Greenwood Press, 1987), and [650] *Records of the Presidency: Presidential Papers and Libraries from Washington to Reagan,* by Frank L. Schick, Renee Schick, and Mark Carroll (Phoenix: Oryx Press, 1989).

A researcher in American history should be aware of the voluminous publication projects of university and other presses, some of them ongoing, for the papers of such presidents as Washington, the Adamses, Jefferson, Madison, Jackson, Polk, Lincoln, Theodore Roosevelt, and Wilson. Plans are afoot to issue the series on the Founding Fathers on CD-ROMs in full text, including documents printed in the published volumes and those assembled but not yet printed.

Federal Employees

Personnel data on employees of the federal government are provided in [651] *Official Register of the United States,* 1816–1959, which was published biennially from 1816 to 1921 and then annually. It was issued by the Department of State 1816–1861, the Department of the Interior 1861–1905, the Bureau of the Census 1907–1932, and finally by the Civil Service Commission until it ceased publication in 1959. Its latest subtitle was *Persons Occupying Administrative and Supervisory Positions in Legislative, Executive and Judicial Branches of Federal Government and in the District of Columbia Government.*

The Federal Census

The censuses of the United States, now conducted by the Bureau of the Census in the Department of Commerce, provide extensive statistical data on population, economic matters, social conditions, and other subjects at ten-year intervals beginning in 1790. For recent decades the published material is voluminous, but it can be tracked down in [652] *Bureau of the Census Catalog of Publications, 1790–1972* (Washington: Bureau of the Census, 1974), which combines and replaces two earlier cumulative catalogs: *Catalog of United States Census Publications, 1790–1945,* by Henry J. Dubester, and *Bureau of the Census Catalog of Publications, 1946–1972*. There have been annual editions of the *Bureau of the Census Catalog* since 1946, and they can be used for the period after 1972 not included in the cumulated catalogs. In 1985 the *Catalog* changed to [653] *Census Catalog and Guide 1985* (Washington: Bureau of the Census, 1985–), which will continue the series. Census publications are listed also in the *Monthly Catalog* [568]. Useful guides to the use of the censuses are [654] *Population Information in Nineteenth Century Census Volumes,* by Suzanne Schulze (Phoenix: Oryx Press, 1983); [655] *Population Information in Twentieth Century Census Volumes, 1900–1940,* by Suzanne Schulze (Phoenix: Oryx Press, 1985); and [656] *Population Information in Twentieth Century Census Volumes, 1950–1980,* by Suzanne Schulze (Phoenix: Oryx Press, 1988). For county boundaries for the census decades superimposed on modern county boundaries, see [657] *Map Guide to the U.S. Federal Censuses, 1790–1920,* by William Thorndale and William Dollarhide (Baltimore: Genealogical Publishing Company, 1982). The actual schedules for each census from 1790 through 1920 are available on microfilm from the National Archives.

The Census Bureau has supplemented its printed reports with machine-readable information, which is available online through CENDATA, covering the 1980 and 1990 censuses. For the 1990 census, the Census Bureau has issued much of its material on CD-ROMs, which are described in a pamphlet, [658] *Census, DC-ROM, and You!* (Washington: Bureau of the Census, 1992).

The Congressional Information Service has issued microfiche collections for all the final publications of the 1970 and 1980 decennial censuses, and it is following the same procedure for the 1990 census as the publications are issued. It publishes an annual [659] *Guide to 1990 US Decennial Census Publications,* which indexes and abstracts the publications as they appear.

Decisions of Federal Courts

The decisions of the Supreme Court of the United States are published in [660] *United States Reports.* The first ninety volumes, although later assigned *United States Reports* volume numbers, are generally cited by the name of the reporter, as follows:

Dallas 1–4	(1790–1800)
Cranch 1–9	(1801–1815)
Wheaton 1–12	(1816–1827)
Peters 1–16	(1828–1842)
Howard 1–24	(1843–1860)
Black 1–2	(1861–1862)
Wallace 1–23	(1863–1874)

In 1875 the title *United States Reports* was adopted and applied to volume 91 and subsequent volumes. Until 1922 the publication of the reports was the responsibility of the reporter, who agreed to furnish a specified number for government distribution; after that date (beginning with vol. 257) the printing has been done at the Government Printing Office and the sale to the public has been handled by the Superintendent of Documents. By December 1992 the series had reached volume 496. Reports of some special federal courts have also been published by the federal government.

An index to Supreme Court decisions is [661] *Supreme Court of the United States, 1789–1980: An Index to Opinions Arranged by Justice,* by Linda A. Blanford and Patricia Russell Evans, sponsored by the Supreme Court Historical Society, 2 vols. (Millwood, N.Y.: Kraus International Publications, 1983).

The briefs and other documents that lie behind a particular Supreme Court decision are often necessary for a full understanding of the case, but these materials in printed form are sometimes difficult to find. Much more complete and convenient for twentieth-century cases are microfiche publication of these records. For cases from 1897 on see the [662] *CIS US Supreme Court Records and Briefs* microfiche collection, issued by the Congressional Information Service.

For reports of federal courts below the Supreme Court, one must rely on commercial publishers. Three series are of importance to the researcher in United States history topics. The first is [663] *Federal Cases,* 30 vols. (St. Paul: West Publishing Company, 1894–1897), which published lower federal court decisions for the period 1789–1880. The [664] *Federal Reporter* (St. Paul: West Publishing Company, 1880–) was published in an initial series of 300 volumes, 1880–1925; a *Second Series,* beginning in 1925 had reached 974 volumes by November 1992. Up to 1932 the *Federal Reporter* reported cases from federal district courts and the Circuit Courts of Appeals, after which date it reported only cases decided by the intermediate courts of appeals. The reports on district courts cases were then furnished by the [665] *Federal Supplement* (St. Paul: West Publishing Company, 1933–). There were 796 volumes by October 1992.

Government Document Libraries

Documents of the federal government are available in many libraries. The government has designated certain libraries across the country as deposit libraries; they receive designated categories of government publications, which they are required to make available for users. These deposit libraries as well as others with federal, state, and international document collections are listed and described in [666] *Directory of Government Document Collections and Librarians,* 6th ed., by Judy Horn, sponsored by the Government Documents Round Table of the American Library Association (Bethesda, Md.: Congressional Information Service, 1991). It includes a list also of libraries that hold documents on special subjects. Since deposit libraries and the categories of documents they hold change, a researcher will need to check local libraries for availability of federal documents in print, in microfiche, and in machine-readable form.

14

The National Archives

The National Archives of the United States is the repository for permanent records of the agencies of the federal government. It is a tremendous concentrated collection of documentary materials for research in United States history, in the form of paper documents, manuscript and printed maps, reels of motion pictures, still pictures, aerial photographs, sound recordings, and machine-readable records. A fascinating and magnificently illustrated popular account of the holdings of the National Archives, which plays up the great variety of material, is [667] *The National Archives of the United States,* by Herman J. Viola (New York: Harry N. Abrams, 1984). It is an admirable introduction, although it is not intended as a guide for research in the Archives.

Prior to the establishment of the National Archives by Congress in 1934, each agency maintained its own records, and many of the documents were poorly organized and badly preserved. With the beginning of the operations of the National Archives in late 1935, the United States at last had a modern archival system for its valuable historical records. At the same time that the organization and maintenance of older records was being pursued, archives personnel also worked toward a broader concept of records management, which included responsibility for the creation of records as well as for their maintenance and disposition.

In 1949, following recommendations of the President's Commission on Organization of the Executive Branch of the Government, the management of the Archives, then designated the National Archives and Records Service (NARS), was placed under the newly created General Services Administration. Later, in April 1985, the National Archives was separated from the General Services Administration and made an independent agency. Its name then was changed to National Archives and Records Administration (NARA).

For many years the archival holdings were concentrated in the National Archives Building in Washington, D.C., which has long since become too small, necessitating the dispersal of records to additional repositories. Now a large proportion of National Archives records are being moved into a new central repository—called Archives II—located at the University of Maryland in College Park; it is scheduled to open in 1994. Eight record clusters (Legislative Branch, Judicial Branch, American Indian related records, Navy, genealogical related records, Old Army, District of Columbia, and Miscellaneous Records) will remain in the old building. Eighteen record clusters (the remaining subject areas) will be concentrated in Archives II, as will nontextual records (cartographic, photographic, sound, and electronic). Microfilm holdings will be divided between the two locations to correspond with the records in each place. The move will involve the transfer and rearrangement of 1,292,000 cubic feet of records. Researchers will need to check ahead of time to find out precisely where records pertinent to their research topics are located.

Guides to Records

The place to begin planning research in the National Archives is the general [668] *Guide to the National Archives of the United States* (Washington: National Archives and Records Service, 1974). This hefty volume of 884 pages describes briefly the holdings in the various collections of records under six broad categories: general records of the United States government, records of the legislative branch, records of the judicial branch, records of the executive branch (which take up most of the *Guide*), records of or relating to other governments, and other holdings. Within these categories, the records are discussed according to Record Groups, the basic organizational unit of the National Archives. The *Guide* defines a Record Group as follows: "A body of organizationally and functionally related records established with particular regard to the administrative history, complexity, and volume of the records and archives of an agency. A typical record group consists of the records of a bureau or some other comparable unit of an executive department at the bureau level, or the records of an independent agency of somewhat comparable importance in the Government's administrative hierarchy." The groups have been numbered in the order in which the records were accessioned. Some groups are "open," with new documents added from time to time; others are "closed," with no new records expected; new Record Groups are created as occasions demand. The 1974 *Guide to the National Archives* was reprinted in 1987 with an appendix showing added Record

Groups (1970–1977), and a new *Guide* is scheduled for publication at the end of 1993.

For many of the Record Groups, researchers can use inventories, preliminary inventories, and special lists that indicate in detail the collections of documents within the Record Group. If these are available, they are the most useful finding aids to the documents. Published inventories and other finding aids are listed in the *Guide to the National Archives* under appropriate Record Groups, and the National Archives has published a [669] *National Archives Publications Catalog* (Washington: National Archives and Records Administration, 1992), which lists guides, finding aids, microfilm catalogs, and special archival publications. The *National Inventory of Documentary Sources in the United States* [304] in part 1, *Federal Records,* includes 429 current finding aids to National Archives Record Groups, including the preliminary inventories, and also finding aids for materials in the presidential libraries. The staff of the Archives is knowledgeable and helpful in guiding researchers to pertinent records.

For some National Archives material special guides have been published, both by the Archives and by other publishers. These include the following:

[670] *American Women and the U. S. Armed Forces: A Guide to the Records of Military Agencies in the National Archives Relating to American Women,* by Charlotte Palmer Seeley, Virginia C. Purdy, and Robert Gruber (Washington: National Archives and Records Administration, 1992).

[671] *Black History: A Guide to Civilian Records in the National Archives,* by Debra L. Newman (Washington: National Archives Trust Fund Board, 1984).

[672] *Catalog of Machine-Readable Records in the National Archives of the United States* (Washington: National Archives Trust Fund Board, 1977).

[673] *The Confederacy: A Guide to the Archives of the Government of the Confederate States of America,* by Henry Putney Beers (Washington: National Archives and Records Administration, 1986). An unrevised reprint of *Guide to the Archives of the Government of the Confederate States of America,* published in 1968.

[674] *Documenting Alaskan History: Guide to Federal Archives Relating to Alaska,* by George S. Ulibarri (Fairbanks: University of Alaska Press, 1982).

[675] *Federal Records of World War II,* 2 vols. (Washington: National Archives and Records Service, 1950–1951). Vol. 1 deals with civilian agencies; vol. 2, with military agencies.

[676] *Guide to Cartographic Records in the National Archives,* by Herman R. Friis and others, rev. by Charlotte M. Ashby and others (Washington: National Archives and Records Service, 1971).

[677] *A Guide to Civil War Maps in the National Archives,* 2d ed. (Washington: National Archives and Records Administration, 1986).

[678] *Guide to Genealogical Research in the National Archives,* rev. ed. (Washington: National Archives Trust Fund Board, National Archives and Records Administration, 1985).

[679] *Guide to Materials on Latin America in the National Archives of the United States,* by George S. Ulibarri and John P. Harrison (Washington: National Archives and Records Service, 1974; reprinted 1988).

[680] *A Guide to Pre-Federal Records in the National Archives,* by Howard H. Wehmann and Benjamin L. DeWhitt (Washington: National Archives and Records Administration, 1989). Relates to records for the period before March 4, 1789, when the Constitution went into effect.

[681] *Guide to Records in the National Archives of the United States Relating to American Indians,* by Edward E. Hill (Washington: National Archives and Records Service, 1981).

[682] *Guide to the Ford Film Collection in the National Archives,* by Mayfield Bray (Washington: National Archives and Records Service, 1970).

[683] *Guide to the Holdings of the Still Picture Branch of the National Archives,* by Barbara Lewis Burger (Washington: National Archives and Records Administration, 1990).

[684] *Guide to the Records of the United States House of Representatives at the National Archives, 1789–1989,* Bicentennial Edition, by Charles E. Schamel and others (Washington: United States House of Representatives, 1989), designated *House Document* no. 100–245, 100th Congress, 2d session.

[685] *Guide to the Records of the United States Senate at the National Archives, 1789–1989,* Bicentennial Edition, by Robert W. Coren and others (Washington: United States Senate, 1989), designated *Senate Document* no. 100–42, 100th Congress, 2d session.

[686] *A Reference Guide to United States Department of State Special Files,* by Gerald K. Haines (Westport, Conn.: Greenwood Press, 1985). Includes records transferred to the National Archives as well as those still in the Department of State.

[687] *The Union: A Guide to Federal Archives Relating to the Civil War,* by Kenneth W. Munden and Henry Putney Beers (Washington: National Archives and Records Administration, 1986). An unrevised reprint of *Guide to Federal Archives Relating to the Civil War,* published in 1962.

The records of the Continental Congress, now housed in the National Archives as Record Group 360, are accessible through [688] *Index, The Papers of the Continental Congress, 1774–1789,* by John P. Butler, 5 vols. (Washington: Government Printing Office, 1978), which, however, excludes the *Journals.* For them, see [689] *Index, Journals of the Continental Congress, 1774–1789,* by Kenneth E. Harris and Steven D. Tilley (Washington: National Archives and Records Service, 1976).

Researchers need to know, also, that what was formerly the library of the Government Printing Office—the most complete collection of printed federal documents in existence—is now part of the National Archives as Record Group 287, Publications of the U.S. Government (also called printed archives). They are arranged mainly by the agency classification scheme developed by the Superintendent of Documents.

Archival Information System

An Archival Information System (AIS), planned for implementation in 1995, will provide computerized access to National Archives records. A series of modules will permit tracking transactions related to accessioned archival records, provide descriptions of holdings, aid in production of online finding aids, offer controlled vocabularies and other authority files, indicate preservation requirements of holdings, and support other administrative activities. There will be a reference module to support National Archives reference activities, including research work of the public; it will allow staff and researchers to conduct sophisticated online searches of the reference components of AIS. Eventually all inventories and preliminary inventories are to be incorporated into the system.

Regional Archives and Federal Records Centers

The National Archives and Records Administration also maintains and administers other agencies and repositories outside the National Archives Building in Washington and Archives II in College Park, Maryland—all of which are important for many research topics in American history.

There are twelve Regional Archives or branches of the National Archives, which hold archival materials of interest to their regions and which also hold copies of many National Archives microfilmed records. At first called Archives Branches, in 1988 they were renamed Regional Archives. They are located as follows:

National Archives—New England Region
> Waltham, Massachusetts
>> Serves Connecticut, Maine, Massachusetts, New Hampshire, Rhode Island, and Vermont.

National Archives—Northeast Region
> New York, New York
>> Serves New Jersey, New York, Puerto Rico, and the Virgin Islands.

National Archives—Mid-Atlantic Region
> Philadelphia, Pennsylvania
>> Serves Delaware, Pennsylvania, Maryland, Virginia, and West Virginia.

National Archives—Southeast Region
> East Point, Georgia
>> Serves Alabama, Georgia, Florida, Kentucky, Mississippi, North Carolina, South Carolina, and Tennessee.

National Archives—Great Lakes Region
> Chicago, Illinois
>> Serves Illinois, Indiana, Michigan, Minnesota, Ohio, and Wisconsin.

National Archives—Central Plains Region
> Kansas City, Missouri
>> Serves Iowa, Kansas, Missouri, and Nebraska.

National Archives—Southwest Region
> Fort Worth, Texas
>> Serves Arkansas, Louisiana, New Mexico, Oklahoma, and Texas.

National Archives—Rocky Mountain Region
  Denver, Colorado
    Serves Colorado, Montana, North Dakota, South Dakota, Utah,
    and Wyoming.
National Archives—Pacific Southwest Region
  Laguna Niguel, California
    Serves Arizona, 11 southern California counties, and Clark
    County, Nevada.
National Archives—Pacific Sierra Region
  San Bruno, California
    Serves northern California, Hawaii, Nevada (except Clark
    County), and the Pacific Ocean area.
National Archives—Pacific Northwest Region
  Seattle, Washington
    Serves Idaho, Oregon, and Washington.
National Archives—Alaska Region
  Anchorage, Alaska
    Serves Alaska.

The materials in the first eleven of these regional institutions (National Archives—Alaska Region was established only in 1990) are described in [690] *The Archives: A Guide to the National Archives Field Branches,* by Loretto Dennis Szucs and Sandra Hargreaves Luebking (Salt Lake City: Ancestry Publishing, 1988). In addition, for each of the eleven branches the National Archives and Records Administration in 1989 published a brief printed introduction, entitled [691] *Guide to Records in the National Archives—New England Region* [and so on for each branch] and in 1990 a comparable set of special lists entitled [692] *Microfilm Publications in the National Archives—New England Region* [and so on]. There is also a comprehensive listing, [693] *National Archives Microfilm Publications in the Regional Archives System,* Special List 45 (Washington: National Archives and Records Administration, 1990).

In general, each of the Regional Archives is located at one of the Federal Records Centers, which are maintained by NARA. The records in the centers are still under the control of the agencies that produced them, but the Office of Federal Records Centers of the National Archives and Records Administration provides economical storage and offers reference service for these active and semiactive federal records to both the agencies themselves and the public. About 5 percent of the records are permanent records, which will ultimately be transferred to the National Archives.

Of special importance for biographical information is the National Personnel Records Center (NPRC), housed in two locations in St. Louis, Missouri, one for records of former members of the armed forces and one for records of former federal civilian employees.

The Washington National Records Center at Suitland, Maryland, which houses an overflow of records from the National Archives Building, will be closed with the opening of Archives II and its records relocated at Archives II and the National Archives Building.

Presidential Libraries

The National Archives and Records Administration is also charged with the presidential libraries, beginning with the Franklin Delano Roosevelt Library at Hyde Park, New York, in 1939. These libraries, built with private funds but maintained and operated by the National Archives, contain massive files relating to the administration of each of the presidents represented. Presidential libraries have now been established for Herbert Hoover (West Branch, Iowa), Harry S. Truman (Independence, Missouri), Dwight D. Eisenhower (Abilene, Kansas), John F. Kennedy (Boston, Massachusetts), Lyndon B. Johnson (Austin, Texas), Gerald R. Ford (Ann Arbor, Michigan), Jimmy Carter (Atlanta, Georgia), Richard Nixon (Whittier, California), and Ronald Reagan (Simi Valley, California).

A listing of manuscript collections, microfilm, and oral histories in the first seven presidential libraries is provided in [694] *A Guide to Manuscripts in the Presidential Libraries,* by Dennis A. Burton, James B. Rhoads, and Raymond W. Smock (College Park, Md.: Research Materials Corporation, 1985). Information on the presidential libraries is included also in *Presidential Libraries and Collections* [649] and *Records of the Presidency: Presidential Papers and Libraries from Washington to Reagan* [650].

National Archives Microfilm

Many of the records in the National Archives have been microfilmed under an ongoing microfilming program. The reels are available for use at the National Archives Building and at Archives II (where researchers are asked to use the microfilm rather than the original records as a preservation measure); they can be purchased from the National Archives, and many of the microfilmed series have been deposited at the Regional Archives for the use of researchers. In addition, a good many university libraries have considerable holdings of this microfilm.

The various collections for which microfilm exists are listed in [695] *National Archives Microfilm Resources for Research: A Comprehensive Catalog,* rev. ed. (Washington: National Archives and Records Administration, 1990). The M or T identification numbers of the microfilm publications are indicated as well as the dates covered and the number of reels. For most of the M series the National Archives has published descriptive pamphlets, which give an introduction to the material and a table of contents to the reels.

In addition, there is a series published by the National Archives Trust Fund Board, in which each volume bears the title [696] *Select Catalog of National Archives Microfilm Publications.* Included are catalogs for American Indians (1984), black studies (1984), genealogical and biographical research (1984), immigrant and passenger arrivals (1984), military service records (1985), diplomatic records (1986), and federal court records (1987). A similar group, somewhat smaller in scope, with each volume titled [697] *A Select List of National Archives Microform Publications,* includes the South and Southwest (1985), the central states (1985), The Chesapeake/Mid-Atlantic region (1985), New England (1985), and the West (1985). See also *National Archives Microfilm Publications in the Regional Archives Systems* [683].

Prologue

The National Archives since 1969 has published [698] *Prologue: The Journal of the National Archives,* a quarterly that contains articles on a great variety of topics based in large part on National Archives records. *Prologue* publishes lists of new accessions to the Archives and other news about National Archives activities.

15

Local, State, and Regional Materials

Much scholarly work in United States history focuses on the federal government and the national experience, and many bibliographical guides follow this pattern. But states and smaller political units also can be studied, and researchers in American history should be able to make their way through the great mass of materials available for such study. An exhaustive listing of bibliographies and other reference works for local, state and regional history cannot be attempted here because of the multiplicity of entities to be considered, but a researcher might begin by looking at the many bibliographies dealing with state history and state records in the two editions of Beers's *Bibliographies in American History* [124–125].

Guides to Public Documents

The *Harvard Guide to American History* [114], pp. 76–87, provides an excellent survey in its sections on state documents, local government documents, and colonial and confederation records. Of particular value for early periods is [699] *A Guide to the Microfilm Collection of Early State Records,* compiled by William Sumner Jenkins (Washington: Library of Congress, 1950), with a supplement published in 1951. Beginning with the year 1910, the Library of Congress has issued a [700] *Monthly Checklist of State Publications* (Washington: Government Printing Office, 1912–). See also [701] "Current Checklists of State Publications," by Barbara Nelson, *Government Publications Review* 1 (Fall 1973): 109–15. A brief bibliography is [702] "State Publications: A Bibliographic Guide for Academic (and Other) Reference Collections," by Peter Hernon, *Library Journal* 97 (April 15, 1972): 1393–98.

There are a good many reference books dealing with state governments. The following will provide useful information to a researcher.
[703] *Check-List of Legislative Journals of States of the United States of America,* by Grace E. MacDonald (Providence: Oxford Press,

1938), with a supplement compiled by William S. Jenkins, Boston, 1943.

[704] *A Check List of Legislative Journals Issued since 1937 by the States of the United States of America,* by William Russell Pullen (Chicago: American Library Association, 1955).

[705] *Collected Public Documents of the States: A Check List,* by William S. Jenkins (Boston: National Association of State Libraries, 1947).

[706] *Guide to State Legislative Materials,* by Mary L. Fisher, 4th ed. (Littleton, Colo.: Fred B. Rothman, 1988).

[707] *Selected Bibliography on State Government,* 1959–1972, by Regis Koslofsky and others (Lexington, Ky.: Council of State Governments, 1972).

[708] *Selected Bibliography on State Government, 1973–1978,* by Susan A. MacManus (Lexington, Ky.: Council of State Governments, 1979).

[709] *State Law Index: An Index to the Legislation of the States of the United States* (1925–1926—1947–1948), 12 vols. (Washington: Government Printing Office, 1929–1949).

[710] *State Legislatures: A Bibliography,* by Robert U. Goehlert and Frederick W. Musto (Santa Barbara, Calif.: ABC-Clio Information Services, 1985).

[711] *State Publications: A Provisional List of the Official Publications of the Several States of the United States from Their Organization,* by R. R. Bowker, issued in 4 parts (New York: Publishers' Weekly, 1899–1908).

A special series of recent bibliographies of state laws, beginning in 1981, which provides a single sequence of numbered bibliographical entries, began with [712] *Subject Compilations of State Laws: Research Guide and Annotated Bibliography,* by Lynn Foster and Carol Boast (Westport, Conn.: Greenwood Press, 1981). Subsequent publications, compiled by Cheryl Rae Nyberg (sometimes with Carol Boast), carried the bibliography forward with volumes for 1979–1983, 1983–1985, 1985–1988, and 1990–1991. The later volumes were published by Carol Boast and Cheryl Nyberg at Urbana, Ill. Volumes now will appear on an annual basis. It should be noted that the full text of statutes of the fifty states are available through LEXIS and WESTLAW.

For information about checklists of state documents, see [713] *State Document Checklists: A Historical Bibliography,* by Susan L. Dow

(Buffalo: William S. Hein and Company, 1990). Recent reference works published by state governments are listed in [714] *State Government Reference Publications: An Annotated Bibliography,* by David W. Parish, 2d ed. (Littleton, Colo.: Libraries Unlimited, 1981), and [715] *A Bibliography of State Bibliographies, 1970–1982,* by David W. Parish (Littleton, Colo.: Libraries Unlimited, 1985). Similar information is found in [716] *State Bluebooks and Reference Publications: A Selected Bibliography* (Lexington, Ky.: Council of State Governments, 1983), and [717] *State Blue Books, Legislative Manuals, and Reference Publications: A Selective Bibliography,* by Lynn Hellebust (Topeka, Kan.: Government Research Service, 1990). A book intended primarily for government documents librarians but useful also for historians who need to use state documents is [718] *State Publications and Depository Libraries: A Reference Handbook,* by Margaret T. Lane (Westport, Conn.: Greenwood Press, 1981). For municipal reference works, see [719] *Municipal Government Reference Sources: Publications and Collections,* edited for the American Library Association Government Documents Round Table by Peter Hernon and others (New York: R. R. Bowker Company, 1978), which is arranged by states and then cities.

State constitutional conventions have received considerable attention. Bibliographies of pertinent materials are [720] *State Constitutional Conventions, from Independence to the Completion of the Present Union, 1776–1959: A Bibliography,* by Cynthia E. Browne (Westport, Conn.: Greenwood Press, 1973), and [721] *State Constitutional Conventions, Commissions, and Amendments, 1959–1978: An Annotated Bibliography,* 2 vols. (Bethesda, Md.: Congressional Information Service, 1981). The latter replaces supplements to Browne's work prepared by Susan Rice Yarger and Bonnie Canning. The series is carried forward by [722] *State Constitutional Conventions, Commissions, and Amendments, 1979–1988: An Annotated Bibliography* (Bethesda, Md.: Congressional Information Service, 1989).

On the state constitutions themselves, see [723] *The Constitutions of the States: A State by State Guide and Bibliography to Current Scholarly Research,* by Bernard D. Reams, Jr., and Stuart D. Yoak (Dobbs Ferry, N.Y.: Oceana Publications, 1988). Greenwood Press had begun a series entitled Reference Guides to the State Constitutions of the United States, which ultimately is expected to cover all 50 states, with a final volume on common themes and a cumulative index. To date volumes have appeared on the constitutions of Florida (by Talbot D'Alemberte, 1991), New York (by

Peter J. Galie, 1990), Louisiana (by Lee Hargrave, 1990), Tennessee (by Lewis L. Laske, 1990), and New Jersey (by Robert F. Williams, 1990).

Censuses prepared by states, which can augment federal censuses, are described in [724] *State Censuses: An Annotated Bibliography of Censuses of Population Taken after the Year 1790 by States and Territories of the United States,* by Henry J. Dubester (New York: Burt Franklin, 1969; reprint of 1948 ed.).

Locations and brief descriptions of archival holdings are given in [725] *Directory of State and Provincial Archives, 1975,* by John M. Kinney (Austin: Society of American Archivists and Texas State Archives, 1975). Other state and local records can be located in the publications of the Historical Records Survey of the Work Projects Administration, which include 628 volumes of county archival inventories; see *Bibliography of Research Projects Reports* [190]. States are beginning to publish inventories of their own archives. Examples are [726] *Guide to Research Materials in the North Carolina State Archives: Section B, County Records,* 8th rev. ed. (Raleigh, N.C.: Office of Archives and History, 1982), following *Section A, State Agency Records* (1963); [727] *Descriptive Inventory of the Archives of the State of Illinois,* by Victoria Irons and Patricia C. Brennan (Springfield: Illinois State Archives, Office of the Secretary of State, 1978), with a supplement issued in 1985 and an index to the *Descriptive Inventory* issued in 1990; and [728] *Minnesota State Archives: Preliminary Checklist,* by Marion E. Matters (St. Paul: Division of Archives and Manuscripts, Minnesota Historical Society, 1979).

For a list of libraries that have collections of state documents, see *Directory of Government Document Collections and Librarians* [666].

Current data about state governments can be found in [729] *The Book of the States,* 1992–1993 ed. (Lexington, Ky.: Council of State Governments, 1992), a biennial, of which this is vol. 29. Supplements to the volumes give information about state officeholders. See also [730] *Worldmark Encyclopedia of the States,* 2d ed. (New York: Worldmark Press/John Wiley and Sons, 1986).

State, County, and Local History

State histories abound, and they can be located relatively easily through general historical bibliographies and subject bibliographies of books.

The *Harvard Guide* [114], pp. 291–323, offers a useful listing both of state histories and of bibliographies that pertain to the history of specific states, and Beers's *Bibliographies in American History* [124–125] provide further leads. Many individual states have bibliographies that provide historical data. A notable example of state historical bibliographies is the 8-volume series [731] *Bibliographies of New England History,* sponsored by the Committee for a New England Bibliography, which includes the following volumes:

[732] *Connecticut: A Bibliography of Its History,* by Roger Parks (Hanover, N.H.: University Press of New England, 1986).

[733] *Maine: A Bibliography of Its History,* by John D. Haskell, Jr. (Boston: G. K. Hall and Company, 1977).

[734] *Massachusetts: A Bibliography of Its History,* by John D. Haskell, Jr. (Boston: G. K. Hall and Company, 1976).

[735] *New Hampshire: A Bibliography of Its History,* by John D. Haskell, Jr., and T. D. Seymour Bassett (Boston: G. K. Hall and Company, 1979).

[736] *Rhode Island: A Bibliography of Its History,* by Roger Parks (Hanover, N.H.: University Press of New England, 1983).

[737] *Vermont: A Bibliography of Its History,* by T. D. Seymour Bassett (Boston: G. K. Hall and Company, 1981).

[738] *New England: A Bibliography of Its History,* by Roger Parks (Hanover, N.H.: University Press of New England, 1989), which treats the region as a whole.

[739] *New England: Additions to the Six State Bibliographies,* by Roger Parks (Hanover, N.H.: University Press of New England, 1989).

Other state bibliographies that might contain references of use to a historian are the following:

[740] *Melvin Ricks' Alaska Bibliography: An Introductory Guide to Alaskan Historical Literature,* edited by Stephen W. Haycox and Betty J. Haycox (Portland, Ore.: Binford and Mort, for the Alaska Historical Commission, 1977).

[741] *Alaska: A Bibliography, 1570–1970, with Subject Index,* by Elsie A. Tourville (Boston: G. K. Hall and Company, 1974).

[742] *Arizona Gathering II, 1950–1969: An Annotated Bibliography,* by Donald M. Powell (Tucson: University of Arizona Press, 1973).

[743] *Sources and Readings in Arizona History: A Checklist of Literature Concerning Arizona's Past,* edited by Andrew Wallace (Tucson: Arizona Pioneers' Historical Society, 1965).

[744] *A Bibliography of the History of California and the Pacific West, 1510–1906*, by Robert Ernest Cowan, new ed. (San Francisco: Book Club of California, 1914).

[745] *A Bibliography of California Bibliographies*, by Francis J. Weber (Los Angeles: Ward Ritchie Press, 1968).

[746] *A Guide to the History of California*, by Doyce B. Nunis, Jr., and Gloria Ricci Lathrop (Westport, Conn.: Greenwood Press, 1989).

[747] *Colorado Bibliography*, by Bohdan S. Wynar (Littleton, Colo.: Libraries Unlimited, for the National Society of Colonial Dames of America in the State of Colorado, 1980).

[748] *A Bibliography of Delaware through 1960*, by H. Clay Reed and Marion Björnson Reed (Newark: University of Delaware Press, for the Institute of Delaware History and Culture, 1966).

[749] *Florida History: A Bibliography*, by Michael H. Harris (Metuchen, N.J.: Scarecrow Press, 1972).

[750] *A Guide to the History of Florida*, by Paul S. George (Westport, Conn.: Greenwood Press, 1989).

[751] *Georgia History: A Bibliography*, by John Eddins Simpson (Metuchen, N.J.: Scarecrow Press, 1976).

[752] *A Bibliography of the Writings on Georgia History, 1900–1970*, by Arthur Ray Rowland and James E. Dorsey, rev. ed. (Spartanburg, S.C.: Reprint Company, 1978). An enlarged edition of a book originally published by Rowland in 1966.

[753] *A Guide to the History of Illinois*, by John Hoffman (Westport, Conn.: Greenwood Press, 1991).

[754] *Iowa History Reference Guide*, by William J. Petersen (Iowa City: State Historical Society of Iowa, 1952).

[755] *Iowa History and Culture: A Bibliography of Materials Published between 1952 and 1986*, by Patricia Dawson and David Hudson (Ames: State History Society of Iowa and Iowa State University Press, 1989), which updates William J. Petersen's work.

[756] *Kansas History: An Annotated Bibliography*, by Homer E. Socolofsky and Virgil W. Dean (Westport, Conn.: Greenwood Press, 1992).

[757] *A Bibliography of Kentucky History*, by J. Winston Coleman, Jr. (Lexington: University of Kentucky Press, 1949).

[758] *A Guide to the History of Louisiana*, by Light Townsend Cummins and Glen Jeansonne (Westport, Conn.: Greenwood Press, 1982).

[759] *A Selected Bibliography of Scholarly Literature on Colonial Louisiana and New France,* by Glenn R. Conrad and Carl A. Brasseaux (Lafayette, La.: Center for Louisiana Studies, University of Southwestern Louisiana, 1982).

[760] *Seventeenth Century Maryland: A Bibliography,* by Elizabeth Baer (Baltimore: John Work Garrett Library, 1949).

[761] *A Guide to the History of Massachusetts,* by Martin Kaufman, John W. Ifkovic, and Joseph Carvalho III (Westport, Conn.: Greenwood Press, 1988).

[762] *A Selective Bibliography of Important Books, Pamphlets, and Broadsides Relating to Michigan History,* by Albert Harry Greenly (Lunenburg, Vt.: Stinehour Press, 1958).

[763] *Reference Guide to Minnesota History: A Subject Bibliography of Books, Pamphlets, and Articles in English,* by Michael Brook (St. Paul: Minnesota Historical Society, 1974), with a supplement issued in 1983.

[764] *Nevada, an Annotated Bibliography: Books and Pamphlets Relating to the History and Development of the Silver State,* by Stanley W. Paher (Las Vegas: Nevada Publications, 1980).

[765] *Politics and Government of New Jersey, 1900–1980: An Annotated Bibliography,* by Benjamin R. Beede and Anne Brugh (Newark: New Jersey Historical Society, 1989).

[766] *A Guide to Materials Bearing on Cultural Relations in New Mexico,* by Lyle Saunders (Albuquerque: University of New Mexico Press, 1944).

[767] *Sources for New Mexican History, 1821–1848,* by Daniel Tyler (Santa Fe: Museum of New Mexico Press, 1984). Identifies manuscript and contemporary printed materials for the period.

[768] *New York: A Guide to Information and Reference Sources, 1979–1986,* by Manuel D. Lopez (Metuchen, N.J.: Scarecrow Press, 1987), which is divided between New York State and New York City.

[769] *A Bibliography of North Carolina, 1589–1956,* by Mary Lindsay Thornton (Chapel Hill: University of North Carolina Press, 1958).

[770] *Reference Guide to North Dakota History,* by Dan Rylance, and *North Dakota Literature,* by J. F. S. Smeall (Grand Forks: Chester Fritz Library, University of North Dakota, 1979).

[771] *Bibliography of Pennsylvania History,* by Norman B. Wilkinson, S. K. Kent, and Donald H. Kent (Harrisburg: Pennsylvania Histori-

cal and Museum Commission, 1957). A supplement, by Carol Wall, was published in 1976. Subsequent volumes, by John B. B. Trussell, Jr., carry additions through 1979.

[772] *Bibliography of South Carolina, 1563–1950*, by Robert J. Turnbull, 6 vols. (Charlottesville, University of Virginia Press, 1956–1960). A posthumous work reproduced from typescript. The 6th vol. is an index.

[773] *Tennessee History: A Bibliography*, by Sam B. Smith (Knoxville: University of Tennessee Press, 1974).

[774] *Basic Texas Books: An Annotated Bibliography of Selected Works for a Research Library*, by John H. Jenkins (Austin: Jenkins Publishing Company, 1983). A revised edition, published by the Texas State Historical Association, Austin, was published in 1987.

[775] *Bibliography of Texas, 1795–1845*, by Thomas W. Streeter, 3 parts in 5 vols. (Cambridge: Harvard University Press, 1955–1960).

[776] *A Guide to the History of Texas*, by Light Townsend Cummins and Alvin R. Bailey, Jr. (Westport, Conn.: Greenwood Press, 1988).

[777] *Bibliography of Virginia History since 1865*, by Lester Jesse Cappon (Charlottesville: Institute for Research in the Social Sciences, University of Virginia, 1930).

The *Guides* published by Greenwood Press listed above are the beginning of a series on the 50 states called Reference Guides to State History and Research.

An up-to-date, carefully produced list of county histories is [778] *A Bibliography of American County Histories*, by P. William Filby (Baltimore: Genealogical Publishing Company, 1985), which largely supersedes the earlier bibliographies by Clarence Stewart Peterson. It lists approximately 5,000 histories.

An extensive bibliography of local histories is [779] *United States Local Histories in the Library of Congress: A Bibliography*, by Marion J. Kaminkow, 4 vols. (Baltimore: Magna Carta Book Company, 1975). A supplement issued as vol. 5 was published in 1976. A bibliography of an extensive collection in the William Chiles Cox Memorial Foundation Library, Tucson, Arizona, is [780] *Shelf List and Catalogue of the Cox Library: A Collection of Local Histories and Biographies*, by Virginia E. Laughlin and Linda J. Pixley (Tucson: Cox Library, 1963). A guide to a microfilmed collection of these materials, plus city directories in the same library, is [781] *The Cox Library: County, State, and Local Histories: A Microfilm Offering from Americana Unlimited* (Tucson: Americana Unlimited, 1974). See also *Dictionary Catalog of the Local History and Genealogy Division,* New York Public Library [45]. For other state, county, and local histories, see the extensive listing in [782] *Bibliographer's Manual of American History, Containing an Account of All State, Territory, Town and County Histories,* by Thomas Lindsley Bradford and Stan. V. Henkels, 5 vols. (Philadelphia: Stan. V. Henkels and Company, 1907–1910). Items are arranged alphabetically by author; vol. 5 is a general index. A useful compilation is *Cities and Towns in American History: A Bibliography of Doctoral Dissertations* [445].

Much state and local history appears in the publications of state and local historical societies. An early exhaustive work is [783] *Bibliography of American Historical Societies (the United States and the Dominion of Canada),* by Appleton Prentiss Clark Griffin, 2d ed., *Annual Report of the American Historical Association for the Year 1905,* vol. 2 (Washington: Government Printing Office, 1907), which lists items in the collections and other publications of historical societies, with a detailed subject and author index. Historical society publications are given in [784] *Directory of State and Local History Periodicals,* by Milton Crouch and Hans Raum (Chicago: American Library Association, 1977). See also [785] *Directory of Historical Organizations in the United States and Canada,* 14th ed., by Mary Bray Wheeler (Nashville: American Association for State and Local History, 1990).

An organization that is devoted to the study of state and local history and that issues books and technical manuals about such study is the American Association for State and Local History, which now has headquarters in Nashville. It publishes the bimonthly [786] *History News.*

Regional Reference Works

American history is often considered regionally, and regions or sections have been singled out for bibliographical treatment. General bibliographies usually have regions among their classification systems. See, for example, *Writings on American History* [105] and the items in Beers's *Bibliographies in American History* [124–125]. Regional imprints have been given special attention; they are noted above in numbers [188] to [190]. A series of essays, edited by John C. Larsen, appears in [787] *Researcher's Guide to Archives and Regional History Sources* (Hamden, Conn.: Library Professional Publications, Shoe String Press, 1988). See also [788] *Region and Regionalism in the United States: A Source Book for the Humanities and Social Sciences,* by Michael Steiner and Clarence Mondale (New York: Garland Publishing, 1988), which deals with regions as a concept and as an object of study.

The American West (including such subdivisions as the Southwest, the Spanish Borderlands, the Pacific Basin, and the Pacific Northwest) is richest of all the sections in bibliographical guides, many of which are listed in the first edition of this *Handbook* [113], pp. 215–18. Two recent bibliographies are [789] *The American West: A Narrative Bibliography and a Study in Regionalism,* by Charles F. Wilkinson (Niwot, Colo.: University Press of Colorado, 1989), and [790] *BorderLine: A Bibliography of the United States–Mexico Borderlands,* by Barbara G. Valk (Los Angeles: UCLA American Center Publications; Riverside: UC MEXUS, University of California Consortium on Mexico and the United States, 1988).

The South also is treated separately in bibliographical works. See, for example, [791] *The American South: An Historical Bibliography,* by Jessica Brown, 2 vols. (Santa Barbara, Calif.: ABC-Clio, 1985), and [792] *The Urban South: A Bibliography,* by Catherine L. Brown (Westport, Conn.: Greenwood Press, 1989).

A number of biographical directories and similar guides pertain specifically to state and territorial governors, to mayors, and to members of state legislatures or local figures. In addition, many states have prepared biographical dictionaries of important men and women in state history. Some of them are scholarly publications on the order of the *Dictionary of American Biography* [463]; others, usually older ones, are often compilations of data without critical appraisal. A good many of the old county histories are largely biographical in nature.

16

Guides to Legal Sources

Legal records are important for historians as well as for political scientists and lawyers, and legal history is a developing branch of American history. A good introduction to the subject, with extensive bibliographical citations, is [793] *The Literature of American Legal History,* by William E. Nelson and John Phillip Reid (New York: Oceana Publications, 1985), which collects and supplements articles surveying American legal history that were published since 1962 in the *Annual Survey of American Law.*

Even historians who do not concentrate on legal matters have need for some acquaintance with legal materials. A widely used guide to legal research, intended for law students but of use also for historians who need to venture into legal sources, is [794] *Fundamentals of Legal Research,* by J. Myron Jacobstein and Roy M. Mersky, 5th ed. (Westbury, N.Y.: Foundation Press, 1990), which is a successor to Ervin H. Pollock's work of the same title. Chapter 22, "Computer-Assisted Legal Research and Microtext," pp. 441–59, will be helpful to researchers using new machine-readable sources. Jacobstein and Mersky have also published [795] *Legal Research Illustrated: An Abridgment of Fundamentals of Legal Research,* 5th ed. (Westbury, N.Y.: Foundation Press, 1990). Another treatise is [796] *How to Find the Law,* 9th ed., by Morris Cohen, Robert C. Berring, and Kent C. Olson (St. Paul: West Publishing Company, 1989), which also deals with computer-based research methods. See, too, the briefer [797] *Legal Research in a Nutshell,* 5th ed., by Morris L. Cohen and Kent C. Olson (St. Paul: West Publishing Company, 1992), which reflects the transition in legal research from traditional printed sources to computerized research. These guides and, indeed, most reference books dealing with legal sources are written for law students or lawyers, and historians using them must make allowance for that fact. Historians' interests and needs are different from those of lawyers, but with a little adaptation, lawyers' guides can also benefit historians.

Government Documents

The basic materials for United States legal history are the documents of the federal government (and comparable documents of state governments). Guides to these sources are described in chapter 13, "Printed Documents of the Federal Government," chapter 14, "The National Archives," and chapter 15, "Local, State, and Regional Materials." The various guides, bibliographies, and indexes listed there will direct researchers to the essential primary sources.

Bibliographies and Other Guides

There is a wide variety of reference works that direct researchers to legal materials, including bibliographies of bibliographies, library catalogs, lists of early records, guides for legislative histories, and numerous general and special bibliographies.

Two retrospective bibliographies are useful because of their comprehensive nature. One is [798] *A Comprehensive Bibliography of American Constitutional and Legal History, 1896–1979,* by Kermit L. Hall, 5 vols. (Millwood, N.Y.: Kraus International Publications, 1984). It has more than 68,000 entries under broad subject categories, although most items are entered under more than one category; vol. 5 consists of author and subject indexes. A *Supplement, 1980–1987,* was published in 2 vols. in 1991. The other is [799] *Law Books, 1876–1981: Books and Serials on Law and Its Related Subjects,* 4 vols. (New York: R. R. Bowker Company, 1981). This work has been updated beginning in 1982 by Bowker's [800] *Law Books and Serials in Print.* In 1988 a new cumulation was published that included entries for microfiche, audio and video cassettes, software, and online databases. The current edition is [801] *Law Books and Serials in Print 1992: A Multimedia Sourcebook,* 3 vols. (New York: R. R. Bowker, 1992). It appears annually.

Other selected works of value to historical researchers are the following.

[802] *The Administration of Justice in the Courts: A Selected Annotated Bibliography,* by Fannie J. Klein, 2 vols. (Dobbs Ferry, N.Y.: Oceana Publications, 1976).

[803] *American Judicial Proceedings First Printed before 1801: An Analytical Bibliography,* by Wilfred J. Ritz (Westport, Conn.: Greenwood Press, 1984).

[804] *American Legal Literature: A Guide to Selected Legal Resources,* by Bernard D. Reams, Jr., James M. Murray, and Margaret H. McDermott (Littleton, Colo.: Libraries Unlimited, 1985).

[805] *A Bibliography of Bibliographies of Legal Material,* by Margaret A. Howell (Woodbridge, N.J., 1969). A supplement for 1969–1971 was published in 1972.

[806] *Court Organization and Administration: A Bibliography,* by Dorothy Campbell Tompkins (Berkeley: Institute of Governmental Studies, University of California, Berkeley, 1973).

[807] *Dictionary Catalog of the Columbia University Law Library,* 28 vols. (Boston: G. K. Hall and Company, 1969). A supplement of 7 vols. was published in 1973 and another of 4 vols. in 1977.

[808] "Historical Studies in United States Legal History, 1950–1959: Bibliography of Articles Published in Scholarly Non-Law Journals," by Doyce B. Nunis, Jr., *American Journal of Legal History* 7 (January 1963): 1–27.

[809] *Historic Preservation Law: An Annotated Bibliography,* by Ellen L. Kettler and Bernard D. Reams, Jr. (Washington: Preservation Press, National Trust for Historic Preservation in the United States, 1976).

[810] *Imported Eighteenth-Century Law Treatises in American Libraries, 1700–1799,* by Herbert A. Johnson (Knoxville: University of Tennessee Press, 1978).

[811] *Legal Ethics: An Annotated Bibliography and Resource Guide,* by Frederick A. Elliston and Jane van Schaick (Littleton, Colo.: Fred B. Rothman and Company, 1984).

[812] *U.S. Constitution: A Guide to Information Sources,* by Earlean M. McCarrick (Detroit: Gale Research Company, 1980).

There are, in addition, some useful bibliographic guides to research in the law of individual states.

Two special areas that are passed over here but for which there is extensive material are criminal justice (including juvenile delinquency) and human rights. Sources for these subjects can be traced in *Guide to Reference Books* [8] and in other general bibliographies as well as in legal bibliographies. For American Indian law see [813] *Felix S. Cohen's Handbook of Federal Indian Law,* 1882 ed. (Charlottesville, Va.: Michie Bobbs-Merrill, 1982), which is based on the classic work [814] *Handbook of Federal Indian Law,* by Felix D. Cohen (Washington: Government Printing Office, 1942).

Indexes to Periodical Literature

An immense literature on legal topics exists, largely in the law journals published by American law schools, and some of it is valuable for historical research. Access to the articles is facilitated by special indexes.

[815] *Current Law Index,* 1980– (Foster City, Calif.: Information Access Corporation, 1980–). Sponsored by the American Association of Law Libraries, it indexes more than 700 law periodicals. There are monthly issues, quarterly cumulations, and annual cumulations (now in 2 vols.). It is available online through WESTLAW, LEXIS, and other services, and on CD-ROM as part of LegalTrac.

[816] *Index to Legal Periodicals,* 1908– (New York: H. W. Wilson Company, 1909–). An annual index to 1925; triennial cumulations, 1926–1979; annual cumulations, 1979–. Now issued quarterly. Available online and on CD-ROM. For aid in searching there is *Index to Legal Periodicals: Thesaurus* (New York: H. W. Wilson Company, 1988).

[817] *Index to Periodical Articles Related to Law,* 1958– (Dobbs Ferry, N.Y.: Glanville and other publishers, 1958–). A selective and flexible index covering periodicals not included in the *Index to Legal Periodicals.* Quarterly with annual cumulations; multiyear cumulations have been issued from time to time. In 1989 a *Thirty Year Cumulation,* volumes 1–30 (1958–1988) was published in 4 vols., edited by Roy M. Mersky and J. Myron Jacobstein.

[818] *An Index to Legal Periodical Literature,* 1791–1937, 6 vols. (Boston: Boston Book Company, 1888–1891, and later publishers).

Other Reference Works

Researchers in legal affairs may find useful material on special topics in handbooks and other general reference works. For example, see [819] *The Guide to American Law: Everyone's Legal Encyclopedia,* 12 vols. (St. Paul: West Publishing Company, 1983–1985). A supplementary *Yearbook* was published in 1987 and an annual *Supplement,* 1990–.

Essential, also, are law dictionaries. A classic work is [820] *Black's Law Dictionary: Definitions of the Terms and Phrases of American and English Jurisprudence, Ancient and Modern,* by Henry Campbell Black and others, 6th ed. (St. Paul: West Publishing Company, 1990). A briefer work, aimed especially at law students, is [821] *Law Dictionary,* by

Steven H. Gifis, 3d ed. (New York: Barron's Educational Series, 1991). For legal usage rather than an exhaustive source of definitions, see [822] *A Dictionary of Modern Legal Usage,* by Bryan A. Garner (New York: Oxford University Press, 1987).

Judges and other persons involved in legal matters are the subject of special biographical directories and dictionaries.

Machine-Readable Materials

Law libraries have been in the forefront of the movement to make materials available in computerized form, and the computer is an essential tool for legal research. Two services especially—WESTLAW and LEXIS—offer extensive information, from bibliographies of legal periodical literature to full-text coverage of court cases, the *Congressional Record* and the *Federal Register.* There are discussions of the use of such services in recent guides to legal research (see titles given at the beginning of this chapter), but historians will probably need special help from law librarians in online or CD-ROM searches.

For finding legal materials, as is the case with less specialized history searches, the computer is a supplement not a replacement for traditional printed reference tools. Often an understanding of the printed books is essential for effective use of the electronic reference works, and many useful materials, especially older ones, are not yet available in electronic form.

17

Atlases, Maps, and Geographical Guides

Since historical events are specified not only by time but by place, geographical information is essential for a historian's work. For some topics in United States history, such as discovery, exploration, and expansion, maps are of paramount importance. Spatial relationships can be studied on contemporary maps (many of which have been reproduced in newer editions) or on maps prepared by modern cartographers. In addition, maps are frequently used to display statistical information—population figures, election returns, or economic data, for example, plotted out on base outline maps of the United States.

Historical Atlases

General historical atlases of the United States are valuable reference tools for research in American history. The most important and comprehensive of these is [823] *Atlas of the Historical Geography of the United States,* by Charles O. Paullin, edited by John K. Wright (Washington: Carnegie Institution; New York: American Geographical Society, 1932). It contains maps of the natural environment, reproductions of historic maps from 1492 to 1867, and maps showing Indians, explorations, boundaries, and military operations. There are also numerous statistical maps depicting a variety of political, social, and economic data. An extensive text explains the maps and indicates the sources on which they are based, and the atlas is thoroughly indexed. Another substantial work is [824] *Atlas of American History,* 2d rev. ed. (New York: Charles Scribner's Sons, 1984). It is an updating of the original work edited by James Truslow Adams published in 1943 as an adjunct to the *Dictionary of American History* [928] and of the first revised edition edited by Kenneth T. Jackson (1978). The maps were prepared under the supervision of history specialists, and include, by and large, all the significant place names of American history. The black-and-white maps of the original

"Pennsylvania's Past" section in *The Atlas of Pennsylvania* (Philadelphia: Temple University Press, 1989).

[846] *A Historical Atlas of Texas,* by William C. Pool, maps by Edward Triggs and Lance Wren (Austin: Encino Press, 1975).

[847] *Historical Atlas of Texas,* by A. Ray Stephens and William M. Holmes (Norman: University of Oklahoma Press, 1989).

[848] *Utah History Atlas,* by David E. Miller, 2d ed. (Salt Lake City: The author, 1968).

[849] *A Historical Atlas of Colonial Virginia,* by John S. Hale (Verona, Va.: McClure Press, 1978).

[850] *Historical Atlas of Washington,* by James W. Scott and Roland L. De Lorme (Norman: University of Oklahoma Press, 1988).

Modern photography and printing techniques have made it possible to produce books with reproductions of historic maps. Some that may be of use to researchers in special areas of United States history are listed here.

[851] *America in Maps Dating from 1500 to 1856,* by Egon Klemp (New York: Holmes and Meier, 1976). An oversize volume with excellent reproductions of historic maps.

[852] *Atlas of the Lewis and Clark Expedition,* by Gary E. Moulton (Lincoln: University of Nebraska Press, 1983).

[853] *The Cartography of North America, 1500–1800,* by Pierluigi Portinaro and Franco Knirsch (New York: Facts on File, 1987).

[854] *Early Maps of North America,* by Robert M. Lunny (Newark: New Jersey Historical Society, 1961).

[855] *The Mapping of Ohio: The Delineation of the State of Ohio through the Use of Manuscript Maps, Printed Maps, and Plats, Sketches and Plans from Original Map Makers with a Narrative Which Describes Each Map from Contemporary Sources,* by Thomas H. Smith (Kent, Ohio: Kent State University Press, 1977).

[856] *Mapping the Transmississippi West, 1540–1861,* by Carl Irving Wheat, 5 vols. (San Francisco: Institute of Historical Cartography, 1957–1963). Vol. 5, in two parts, covers the period from the Civil War to the Geological Surveys; although the title remains the same, material is carried into the 1880s.

[857] *Maps of Texas and the Southwest, 1513–1900,* by James C. Martin and Robert Sidney Martin (Albuquerque: University of New Mexico Press, published for the Amon Carter Museum, 1984). Reproductions of 50 maps, some in color, with commentary.

[858] *Railroad Maps of North America: The First Hundred Years,* by Andrew M. Modelski (Washington: Library of Congress, 1984). Contains 92 maps from the Geography and Map Division of the Library of Congress.

[859] *Rand McNally's Pioneer Atlas of the American West,* historical text by Dale L. Morgan (Chicago: Rand McNally and Company, 1956). Contains facsimile reproductions of maps and indexes from an 1876 atlas.

[860] *The Southeast in Early Maps, with a Check List of Printed and Manuscript Regional and Local Maps of Southeastern North America during the Colonial Period,* by William P. Cumming (Chapel Hill: University of North Carolina Press, 1962).

Still other atlases deal with particular aspects of American history, laying out in graphic form a great deal of information. The wide variety of such publications can be seen from the following examples.

[861] *American Expansion: A Book of Maps,* by Randall D. Sale and Edwin D. Karn (Homewood, Ill.: Dorsey Press, 1962). A map for each census year, with political boundaries of the time, extension of settlement, exploration, and location of land offices.

[862] *Atlas of American Indian Affairs,* by Francis Paul Prucha (Lincoln: University of Nebraska Press, 1990).

[863] *Atlas of American Wars,* by Richard Natkiel, text by John Kirk and John Westwood (Greenwich, Conn.: Arch Cape Press, 1986).

[864] *Atlas of American Women,* by Barbara Gimla Shortridge (New York: Macmillan Publishing Company, 1987). Data by states.

[865] *Atlas of Antebellum Southern Agriculture,* by Sam Bowers Hilliard (Baton Rouge: Louisiana State University Press, 1984).

[866] *Atlas of Great Lakes Indian History,* by Helen Hornbeck Tanner (Norman: University of Oklahoma Press, for the Newberry Library, 1987).

[867] *Atlas of Religious Change in America, 1952–1971,* by Peter L. Halvorson and William M. Newman (Washington: Glenmary Research Center, 1978).

[868] *Atlas of Religion Change in America, 1971–1980,* by Peter L. Halvorson and William M. Newman (Atlanta: Glenmary Research Center, 1987).

[869] *Atlas of United States Environmental Issues,* by Robert J. Mason and Mark T. Mattson (New York: Macmillan Publishing Company, 1990).

[870] *Atlas of United States Foreign Relations,* by Harry F. Young, 2d ed. (Washington: United States Department of State, Bureau of Public Affairs, 1985).

[871] *Atlas to Accompany the Official Records of the Union and Confederate Armies* (Washington: Government Printing Office, 1891–1895), with 171 places covering military operations. This atlas has been reprinted as *The Official Atlas of the Civil War,* introduction by Henry Steele Commager (New York: Thomas Yoseloff, 1958), and as *The Official Military Atlas of the Civil War* (New York: Arno Press/Crown Publishers, 1978). See also *Civil War Maps: A Graphic Index to the Atlas to Accompany the Official Records of the Union and Confederate Armies,* by Noel S. O'Reilly, David C. Bosse, and Robert W. Karrow, Jr. (Chicago: Newberry Library, 1987).

[872] *A Comparative Atlas of America's Great Cities: Twenty Metropolitan Regions,* by John S. Adams and Ronald Alber (Minneapolis: University of Minnesota Press and Association of American Geographers, 1976).

[873] *The Great Lakes: An Environmental Atlas and Resource Book,* by Lee Botts and Bruce Krushelnick (Toronto: Environment Canada and joint publishers, 1987).

[874] *The Geography of American Labor and Industrialization, 1865–1908: An Atlas,* by Sari Bennett and Carville Earle (Catonsville: Department of Geography, University of Maryland, Baltimore County, 1980).

[875] *Historical Atlas of Religion in America,* by Edwin Scott Gaustad, rev. ed. (New York: Harper and Row, 1976). Numerous statistical maps, tables, and charts and an extensive explanatory text.

[876] *Historical Atlas of the American West,* by Warren A. Beck and Ynez D. Haase (Norman: University of Oklahoma Press, 1989).

[877] *Oxford Regional Economic Atlas: The United States and Canada,* John D. Chapman and John C. Sherman, advisory editors, 2d ed. (Oxford: Oxford University Press, 1975).

[878] *The Navajo Atlas: Environments, Resources, People, and History of the Diné Bikeyah,* by James M. Goodman (Norman: University of Oklahoma Press, 1982).

[879] *The West Point Atlas of American Wars,* by Vincent J. Esposito, 2 vols. (New York: Frederick A. Praeger, 1959). The two volumes divide at 1900.

[880] *We the People: An Atlas of America's Ethnic Diversity,* by James P. Allen and Eugene J. Turner (New York: Macmillan Publishing Company, 1988). A remarkable display by maps and charts of ethnic data.

[881] *The Women's Atlas of the United States,* by Anne Gibson and Timothy Fast (New York: Facts on File Publications, 1986).

[882] *A Zuni Atlas,* by T. J. Ferguson and E. Richard Hart (Norman: University of Oklahoma Press, 1985).

Political divisions of the United States—such as counties and congressional districts—are difficult to trace historically, yet they sometimes must be sought out to explain some document or to plot out historical data for the researcher's own use. Fortunately, there are now a number of very useful publications to further such work. County boundaries for each decade from 1840 to 1980 are shown in [883] *Historical U.S. County Outline Map Collection, 1840–1980,* Thomas D. Rabenhorst, senior editor (Baltimore: Department of Geography, University of Maryland Baltimore County, 1984). This publication is a portfolio that includes for each decade large maps with county names, plus a number of smaller maps showing the county divisions (but without the names) on which data can be entered. The maps were based upon a series of maps originally produced by the United States Department of Agriculture. A similar collection of maps (by states), which shows county boundaries for each census from 1790 to 1920 superimposed on maps showing current county boundaries is *Map Guide to the U.S. Federal Censuses* [657].

For more detailed information on changing county boundaries in Pennsylvania, New Jersey, Maryland, Delaware, Indiana, Illinois, Michigan, Ohio, Wisconsin, Missouri, Iowa, Minnesota, North Dakota, and South Dakota, see [884] *Historical Atlas and Chronology of County Boundaries, 1788–1980,* edited by John H. Long, 5 vols. (Boston: G. K. Hall and Company, 1984). The volumes contain about 1000 computer-produced maps from the Historical Boundary Data File at the Newberry Library. This is a continuing series. A source of information on current minor civil divisions is [885] *Township Atlas of the United States,* by Jay Andriot (McLean, Va.: Documents Index, 1991). A book that gives a history of state boundaries is [886] *Boundaries of the United States and the Several States,* by Franklin K. Van Zandt, Geological Survey Professional Paper no. 909 (Washington: Government Printing Office, 1976). It supersedes a similar work published in 1966.

A remarkable recent compilation is [887] *The Historical Atlas of United States Congressional Districts, 1789–1983*, by Kenneth C. Martis (New York: Free Press, 1982). It provides clear outline maps showing congressional districts by congresses, from the 1st to the 97th (1789–1983), with alphabetical lists of members indicating their states and districts and a very informative text. For congressional districts in the early national period, see the maps and accompanying data in [888] *United States Congressional Districts, 1788–1841*, by Stanley B. Parsons, William W. Beach, and Dan Hermann (Westport, Conn.: Greenwood Press, 1978) and in [889] *United States Congressional Districts and Data, 1843–1883*, by Stanley B. Parsons, William W. Beach, and Michael J. Dubin (Westport, Conn.: Greenwood Press, 1986). There is also a series of congressional district atlases, of which the latest is [890] *Congressional District Atlas: 100th Congress of the United States* (Washington: Bureau of the Census, 1985). This is the eleventh in a series of atlases issued periodically since 1960, whenever a number of states have changed congressional district boundaries.

A companion volume to Martis's atlas of congressional districts is [891] *The Historical Atlas of Political Parties in the United States Congress, 1789–1989*, by Kenneth C. Martis (New York: Macmillan Publishing Company, 1989).

Of special value to urban historians are the fire insurance maps produced by the Sanborn Map Company. These large-scale maps, dating from 1867, show the location of commercial, industrial, and residential buildings in some 1,200 cities and towns in the United States, Canada, and Mexico. The largest collection of these maps is in the Library of Congress, which includes 50,000 editions of the maps with an estimated 700,000 individual sheets; other libraries have smaller collections, usually of local or regional maps. See [892] *Fire Insurance Maps in the Library of Congress: Plans of North American Cities and Towns Produced by the Sanborn Map Company* (Washington: Library of Congress, 1981).

Guides to Maps and Atlases

For researchers who need to seek out special maps, there are comprehensive and useful guides, directories, and indexes.

Two up-to-date directories of map collections are [893] *Guide to U.S. Map Resources*, by David A. Cobb, 2d ed. (Chicago: American Library Association, 1990), and [894] *Map Collections in the United States and Canada: A Directory,* 4th ed., by David K. Carrington and Richard W. Stephenson (New York: Special Libraries Association, 1985). A recent directory of map collections throughout the world is [895] *World Directory of Map Collections,* 2d ed., by John A. Wolter, Ronald E. Grim, and David K. Carrington (New York: K. G. Saur, 1986). It has a section on collections in the United States, arranged by states, on pp. 323–77.

Some extensive repositories of maps and other geographical information have printed catalogs or other guides to their holdings, and there are a number of additional guides to such materials. The following works may be of use to a researcher in United States history.

[896] *Alaskan Maps: A Cartobibliography of Alaska to 1900,* by Marvin W. Falk (New York: Garland Publishing, 1983).

[897] *The Bancroft Library, University of California, Berkeley: Index to Printed Maps* (Boston: G. K. Hall and Company, 1964). A supplement was issued in 1975.

[898] *A Bibliography of Printed Battle Plans of the American Revolution, 1775–1795,* by Kenneth Nebenzahl (Chicago: University of Chicago Press, 1975).

[899] *Checklist of Printed Maps of the Middle West to 1900,* Robert W. Karrow, Jr., general editor, 14 vols. in 12 vols. (Boston: G. K. Hall and Company, 1981–1983). A project of the Herman Dunlap Smith Center for the History of Cartography, Newberry Library. A systematic listing of maps of Ohio, Indiana, Michigan, Illinois, Wisconsin, Minnesota, Iowa, Missouri, North Dakota, South Dakota, Nebraska, Kansas, and the Great Lakes and Northern Great Plains regions, with a subject, author, and title index.

[900] *Civil War Maps: An Annotated List of Maps and Atlases in the Library of Congress,* 2d ed. (Washington: Library of Congress, 1989).

[901] *Descriptive Catalog of Maps Published by Congress, 1817–1843,* by Martin P. Claussen and Herman R. Friis (Washington: The authors, 1941). A catalog of maps published in the Congressional Serial Set, 15th–27th congresses, comprising 503 maps scattered throughout vols. 1–429 of the Serial Set. A fuller checklist and index to the maps in the Congressional Serial Set is being prepared by Donna P. Koepp, of the University of Kansas.

[902] *Dictionary Catalog of the Map Division,* The Research Libraries, New York Public Library, 10 vols. (Boston: G. K. Hall and Com-

pany, 1971). Supplemented annually by *Bibliographic Guide to Maps and Atlases* [52].

[903] *Index to Maps in Books and Periodicals,* Map Department, American Geographical Society, 10 vols. (Boston: G. K. Hall and Company, 1968). Supplements were issued in 1971, 1976, and 1987.

[904] *Index to Maps of the American Revolution in Books and Periodicals, Illustrating the Revolutionary War and Other Events of the Period 1763–1789,* by David Sanders Clark (Westport, Conn.: Greenwood Press, 1974).

[905] *A List of Maps of America in the Library of Congress,* by Philip Lee Phillips (Washington: Government Printing Office, 1901).

[906] *Maps and Charts of North America and the West Indies, 1750–1789: A Guide to the Collections in the Library of Congress,* by John R. Sellers and Patricia Molen Van Ee (Washington: Library of Congress, 1981).

[907] *Maps and Charts Published in America before 1800: A Bibliography,* by James C. Wheat and Christian F. Brun, rev. ed., Holland Press Cartographica no. 3 (London: Holland Press, 1978). Originally published by Yale University Press in 1969.

[908] *Maps for America: Cartographic Products of the U.S. Geological Survey and Others,* by Morris M. Thompson, 3d ed. (Washington: U.S. Geological Survey, Department of the Interior, 1987).

[909] *Maps of America in Periodicals before 1800,* by David C. Jolly (Brookline, Mass.: David C. Jolly, 1989).

[910] *Panoramic Maps of Cities in the United States and Canada: A Checklist of Maps in the Collections of the Library of Congress, Geography and Map Division,* 2d ed., by Patrick E. Dempsey (Washington: Library of Congress, 1984). Lists 1,726 panoramic maps of cities in 47 states and in Canada.

[911] *Printed Maps of Utah to 1900: An Annotated Cartobibliography,* by Riley Moore Moffat (Santa Cruz, Calif.: Western Association of Map Libraries, 1981). Lists 303 printed maps of Utah, 1778–1899.

[912] *"Realms of Gold": A Catalogue of Maps in the Library of the American Philosophical Society,* by Murphy D. Smith (Philadelphia: American Philosophical Society, 1991).

[913] *Research Catalog of Maps of America to 1860 in the William L. Clements Library,* University of Michigan, by Douglas W. Marshall, 4 vols. (Boston: G. K. Hall and Company, 1972).

See also *Guide to Cartographic Records in the National Archives*

[676], *Guide to Civil War Maps in the National Archives* [677], *Maps Contained in the Publications of the American Bibliography* [166], and *National Union Catalog: Cartographic Materials* [34].

Dictionaries and Gazetteers

If one needs to check a place name for identification, spelling, or pronunciation, a dictionary or gazetteer is the best place to look. A standard work of this nature is [914] *Webster's New Geographical Dictionary,* (Springfield, Mass.: Merriam-Webster, 1988). Of similar use are [915] *The Columbia Lippincott Gazetteer of the World, with 1961 Supplement,* edited by Leon E. Seltzer (New York: Columbia University Press, by arrangement with J. B. Lippincott Company, 1962); [916] *The International Geographic Encyclopedia and Atlas* (Boston: Houghton Mifflin Company, 1979); [917] *The National Gazetteer of the United States Concise, 1990* (Washington: Government Printing Office, 1990), a select list of about 42,000 geographical names prepared by the U.S. Geological Survey in cooperation with the U.S. Board of Geographic Names; and [918] *Place Guide,* by Donna Andriot and others (McLean, Va.: Documents Index, 1990). For those who want more comprehensive information there is [919] *Omni Gazetteer of the United States of America: Providing Name, Location, and Identification for Nearly 1,500,000 Populated Places, Structures, Facilities, Locales, Historic Places, and Geographic Features in the Fifty States, the District of Columbia, Puerto Rico, and U.S. Territories,* by Frank R. Abate, 11 vols. (Detroit: Omnigraphics, 1991). There are 9 volumes treating regional groupings of states, a full index volume, and a final volume of other reference material.

See also [920] *The Encyclopedia of Historic Places,* by Courtlandt Canby, 2 vols. (New York: Facts on File Publications, 1984); [921] *Illustrated Dictionary of Place Names, United States and Canada,* by Kelsie B. Harder (New York: Van Nostrand Reinhold Company, 1976); and [922] *American Place-Names: A Concise and Selective Dictionary for the Continental United States of America,* by George R. Stewart (New York: Oxford University Press, 1970), which gives the origins of place names. There is also a [923] *Bibliography of Place-Name Literature: United States and Canada,* 3d ed., by Richard B. Sealock, Margaret M. Sealock, and Margaret S. Powell (Chicago: American Library Association, 1982).

Geographical Bibliographies

The disciplines of geography and history are drawing closer together, and geographers now study many of the same topics and events that interest historians, adding a spatial dimension to the work. It can be helpful for historians, therefore, on occasion to search geographical literature. For aid in that task, see [924] *A Geographical Bibliography for American Libraries,* edited by Chauncy D. Harris and others (Washington: Association of American Geographers and National Geographical Society, 1985); [925] *Historical Geography of the United States: A Guide to Information Sources,* by Ronald E. Grim (Detroit: Gale Research Company, 1982); and [926] *Bibliography of Geography,* Part II: *Regional,* vol. 1, *The United States of America,* by Chauncy D. Harris (Chicago: Department of Geography, University of Chicago, 1984), which is essentially a bibliography of bibliographies. See also [927] *The History of Modern Geography: An Annotated Bibliography of Selected Works,* by Gary S. Dunbar (New York: Garland Publishing, 1985). The author published *Corregenda and Addenda* in 1987.

18

Dictionaries and Encyclopedias

A researcher may frequently need to use reference works, not to search out sources for research, but simply to check a name or date or confirm the facts about a historical event. There are a number of such works that are very useful and convenient to have at hand.

Dictionaries of American History

A standard work is [928] *Dictionary of American History,* rev. ed., 8 vols. (New York: Charles Scribner's Sons, 1976–1978). This work, originally edited in five volumes (1940) by James Truslow Adams, has seven volumes of entries (7,200 signed entries by some 800 contributors) and an eighth volume containing an analytical index. A short abridgment in one volume is [929] *Scribner Desk Dictionary of American History* (New York: Charles Scribner's Sons, 1984). A somewhat longer abridgment is the one-volume [930] *Concise Dictionary of American History* (New York: Charles Scribner's Sons, 1988).

There are other one-volume dictionaries or handbooks that can serve as quick reference guides. Some useful ones are listed here.

[931] *Encyclopedia of American History,* by Richard B. Morris and Jeffrey B. Morris, 6th ed. (New York: Harper and Row, 1982).

[932] *An Encyclopedic Dictionary of American History,* by Howard L. Hurwitz (New York: Washington Square Press, 1974).

[933] *The New Dictionary of American History,* by Michael Martin and Leonard Gelber, rev. ed., by A. W. Littlefield (New York: Philosophical Library, 1965).

[934] *The Oxford Companion to American History,* by Thomas H. Johnson (New York: Oxford University Press, 1966).

[935] *The Reader's Companion to American History,* by Eric Foner and John A. Garraty (Boston: Houghton Mifflin Company, 1991).

[936] *Webster's Guide to American History: A Chronological, Geographical, and Biographical Survey and Compendium,* by Charles

Van Doren and Robert McHenry (Springfield, Mass.: G. and C. Merriam Company, 1971).

Similar to these brief encyclopedias and dictionaries are date books or almanacs, which emphasize the chronology. A work of this sort is [937] *The Almanac of American History,* Arthur M. Schlesinger, Jr., general editor (New York: Putnam Publishing Group, 1983), which is divided into five chronological periods, each the responsibility of a consulting editor. See also [938] *The Encyclopedia of American Facts and Dates,* by Gorton Carruth, 8th ed. (New York: Harper and Row, 1987).

Students of American history may also find occasion to use the one-volume [939] *An Encyclopedia of World History: Ancient, Medieval, and Modern, Chronologically Arranged,* by William L. Langer, 5th ed., rev. and enl. (Boston: Houghton Mifflin Company, 1972). There is an illustrated version of this handbook, [940] *The New Illustrated Encyclopedia of World History,* 2 vols. (New York: H. N. Abrams, 1975), which uses the text of the 1972 edition and is profusely illustrated.

General Encyclopedias

Frequently a standard multivolume encyclopedia can furnish background information and other data of use. Traditionally, the most significant of these in English is [941] *The New Encyclopaedia Britannica,* 15th ed., revised, 32 vols. (Chicago: Encyclopaedia Britannica, 1991). The latest edition is divided into *Propaedia: Outline of Knowledge and Guide to the Britannica,* 1 vol.; *Micropaedia: Ready Reference and Index,* 12 vols.; *Macropaedia: Knowledge in Depth,* 17 vols.; and a two-volume index. Historians will also find useful older editions of this encyclopedia, especially the ninth and the eleventh. Other general, up-to-date works are [942] *Collier's Encyclopedia with Bibliography and Index,* 24 vols. (New York: Macmillan Educational Company, 1991); and [943] *Encyclopedia Americana, International Edition,* 30 vols. (Danbury, Conn.: Grolier, 1991). Short general encyclopedias, valuable for quick checking of information, are [944] *The New Columbia Encyclopedia,* edited by William H. Harris and Judith S. Levey, 4th ed. (New York: Columbia University Press, 1975); and [945] *The Random House Encyclopedia,* James Mitchell, editor in chief, 3d ed. (New York: Random House, 1990).

Two guides for those seeking other encyclopedias, general or classified, are [946] *Anglo-American General Encyclopedias: A Historical Bibliography, 1703–1967*, by S. Padraig Walsh [James Patrick Walsh] (New York: R. R. Bowker Company, 1968); and [947] *Dictionaries, Encyclopedias, and Other Word-Related Books*, by Annie M. Brewer, 4th ed., 2 vols. (Detroit: Gale Research Company, 1988).

Specialized Encyclopedias

Besides the general all-purpose encyclopedias, there are some multivolume works that pertain to special fields or topics. A very useful one for historians is [948] *International Encyclopedia of the Social Sciences*, edited by David L. Sills, 17 vols. (New York: Macmillan Company and Free Press, 1968). A *Biographical Supplement* was published as volume 18 in 1979. An older publication that has not been completely replaced by the newer one is [949] *Encyclopedia of the Social Sciences*, edited by Edwin R. A. Seligman, 15 vols. (New York: Macmillan Company, 1930–1935). There are other sets of encyclopedias dealing with special areas, for example, religion and education.

A good many shorter works dealing with particular subjects are available; they might be useful as handy references to some researchers. Among them are the following:

[950] *The Civil War Dictionary*, by Mark Mayo Boatner III, rev. ed. (New York: McKay Books, 1988).

[951] *Dictionary of American Diplomatic History*, by John E. Findling, 2d ed. (Westport, Conn.: Greenwood Press, 1989).

[952] *Dictionary of American Immigration History*, by Francesco Cordasco (Metuchen, N.J.: Scarecrow Press, 1990).

[953] *Dictionary of Asian American History*, by Hyung-Chan Kim (Westport, Conn.: Greenwood Press, 1986).

[954] *Dictionary of Mexican American History*, by Matt S. Meier and Feliciano Rivera (Westport, Conn.: Greenwood Press, 1981).

[955] *Encyclopedia of American Agricultural History*, by Edward L. Schapsmeier and Frederick H. Schapsmeier (Westport, Conn.: Greenwood Press, 1975).

[956] *Encyclopedia of American Forest and Conservation History*, by Richard C. Davis, 2 vols. (New York: Macmillan Publishing Company, 1983).

[957] *The Encyclopedia of American Religions*, by J. Gordon Melton, 3d ed. (Detroit: Gale Research, 1989).

[958] *The Encyclopedia of Southern History,* edited by David C. Roller and Robert W. Twyman (Baton Rouge: Louisiana State University Press, 1979).

[959] *Encyclopedia of the American Constitution,* Leonard W. Levy, editor in chief, 4 vols. (New York: Macmillan Publishing Company, 1986). A *Supplement I* was published in 1992.

[960] *Encyclopedia of the American Revolution,* by Mark Mayo Boatner III, Bicentennial Edition (New York: David McKay Company, 1974).

[961] *Encyclopedia of Third Parties in the United States,* by Earl R. Kruschke (Santa Barbara, Calif.: ABC-Clio, 1991).

[962] *Harvard Encyclopedia of American Ethnic Groups,* by Stephen Thernstrom (Cambridge: Harvard University Press, 1980).

[963] *Jewish-American History and Culture: An Encyclopedia,* by Jack Fischel and Sanford Pinsker (New York: Garland Publishing, 1992).

[964] *The Negro Almanac: A Reference Work on the African American,* by Harry A. Ploski and James Williams, 5th ed. (Detroit: Gale Research, 1989).

[965] *The Reader's Encyclopedia of the American West,* by Howard R. Lamar (New York: Thomas Y. Crowell Company, 1977).

19

Statistics

Some research topics in United States history rely heavily on quantitative statistics, and it is necessary to acquire techniques of locating and using such data that are beyond the scope of this *Handbook*. But even a researcher in nonstatistical subjects will occasionally need to locate figures on population, economic development, or social conditions. A good place to look for such information is [966] *Historical Statistics of the United States: Colonial Times to 1970*, Bicentennial Edition, 2 vols. (Washington: Bureau of the Census, 1975). The information is taken largely from the [967] *Statistical Abstract of the United States*, which has been published annually by the Bureau of the Census since 1878 and which can also serve to update *Historical Statistics*.

Current statistics sources can be found in two series published by Congressional Information Service: [968] *American Statistics Index: A Comprehensive Guide and Index to the Statistical Publications of the U.S. Government (ASI)*, which began with a retrospective volume covering publications in print as of January 1, 1974; it has annual volumes (a volume of abstracts and a volume of index) and monthly supplements; and [969] *Statistical Reference Index: A Selective Guide to American Statistical Publications from Private Organizations and State Government Sources (SRI)*, which similarly has annual volumes and monthly issues, beginning with an annual for 1980. These materials are available on CD-ROM under the title [970] *Statistical Masterfile*. For other electronic databases, see [971] *Federal Statistical Data Bases: A Comprehensive Catalog of Current Machine-Readable and Online Files*, by William R. Evinger (Phoenix: Oryx Press, 1988).

An extensive guide to statistical publications is [972] *Statistics Sources: A Subject Guide to Data on Industrial, Business, Social, Education, Financial, and Other Topics for the United States and Internationally*, 15th ed., 1992, by Jacqueline Wasserman O'Brien and Steven R. Wasserman, 2 vols. (Detroit: Gale Research Company, 1991). See also [973] *Guide to U.S. Government Statistics, 1990–1991*, by Donna

Andriot, Jay Andriot, and Laurie Andriot (McLean, Va.: Documents Index, 1990); and [974] *State and Local Statistics Sources,* 1st ed., 1990–1991 (Detroit: Gale Research, 1990).

Of use, too, in finding statistics are the following older works:

[975] *Directory of Federal Statistics for Local Areas: A Guide to Sources, 1976* (Washington: Bureau of the Census, 1978). Urban material was updated in an *Urban Update, 1977–1978* (1979).

[976] *Directory of Federal Statistics for States: A Guide to Sources, 1967* (Washington: Bureau of the Census, 1967).

[977] *Directory of Non-Federal Statistics for States and Local Areas: A Guide to Sources, 1969* (Washington: Bureau of the Census, 1970).

The decennial censuses of the United States are a primary source of statistical data. They are discussed in chapter 13.

Statistical data from government and other sources have been extracted by subject matter. Here are examples of such publications.

[978] *Nations within a Nation: Historical Statistics of American Indians,* by Paul Stuart (Westport, Conn.: Greenwood Press, 1987).

[979] *Statistical Handbook on U.S. Hispanics,* by Frank L. Schick and Renee Schick (Phoenix: Oryx Press, 1991).

[980] *Statistical Handbook on Women in America,* by Cynthia Taeuber (Phoenix: Oryx Press, 1991).

20

Picture Sources

Visual materials as well as written texts are necessary for research in American history. The value of pictures as a source of information is increasingly recognized, and there are few topics in the history of the United States that cannot be enriched by use of contemporary illustrations—landscapes, urban scenes, technological developments, political and military events, social and economic activities, important personages, and family and other groupings. And to traditional drawings, paintings, sculptures, and photographs have been added posters, cartoons, motion pictures, videodisks and videotapes, and more. Some histories, indeed, are largely pictorial, and others have sizable portfolios of illustrations. Documentary videos rely heavily, of course, on pictures from the past.

Tracking down usable visuals, however, is not as easy as finding textual documentation, and the reference works that might lead one to appropriate images are few. A researcher must keep an eye open for pictures as research on a topic progresses and most likely will need to inquire in person or by mail at likely depositories, among which state and local historical societies will rank high.

A helpful place to start is [981] *Picture Sources,* 4th ed., by Ernest H. Robl (New York: Special Libraries Association, 1983), which provides descriptions of 980 picture collections including general subject coverage. Unfortunately, the Picture Division of the Special Libraries Association, which produced the work and which intended to keep it up to date with new editions, disbanded in the mid-1980s, and its work stopped. Its quarterly journal, [982] *Picturescope,* begun in 1953 as a newsletter for members and expanded in the 1980s to include valuable articles on particular picture collections and on techniques in the use of pictures, also ceased publication. A work similar to *Picture Sources* is [983] *Picture Researcher's Handbook: An International Guide to Picture Sources—and How to Use Them,* by Hilary Evans and Mary Evans, 3d ed. (Wokingham, England: Van Nostrand Reinhold (UK) Company,

1986). Although it has worldwide coverage, there is a brief section on United States depositories.

For a century and a half, photographs have been a primary means of recording historical events and persons, and they exist in large numbers. An extensive guide to collections is [984] *Stock Photo Deskbook,* by Fred W. McDarrah, 3d ed. (New York: Photo Arts Center, 1989), which provides only broad subject categories but indicates addresses, phone numbers, and FAX numbers, so that the agency or individual holding the photos can be asked for specific information.

An interesting attempt to make photographs, in this case of American Indians, available to researchers was [985] *North American Indians: Photographs from the National Anthropological Archives, Smithsonian Institution,* by Herman Viola (Chicago: University of Chicago Press, 1974), which reproduced about 5,000 photographs on 52 microfiche. Titles and order numbers were supplied, so that glossy prints could be ordered. Unfortunately, no other similar aids to picture research were forthcoming.

Two companion works that locate illustrations printed in monographs, exhibition catalogs, and collection catalogs are [986] *Photography Index: A Guide to Reproductions,* by Pamela Jeffcott Parry (Westport, Conn.: Greenwood Press, 1979), and [987] *Print Index: A Guide to Reproductions,* by Pamela Jeffcott Parry and Kathe Chipman (Westport, Conn.: Greenwood Press, 1983). These have international coverage, but there are some American items; they have subject and title indexes.

Researchers seeking only portraits of historical figures can get substantial help from the old [988] *A.L.A. Portrait Index: Index to Portraits Contained in Printed Books and Periodicals,* by William C. Lane and Nina E. Browne (Washington: Government Printing Office, 1906). Between 35,000 and 45,000 persons are listed. A more recent work is [989] *Dictionary of American Portraits: 4045 Pictures of Important Americans from Earliest Times to the Beginning of the Twentieth Century,* by Hayward Cirker and Blanche Cirker (New York: Dover Publications, 1967), which provides small reproductions of the portraits, arranged alphabetically.

Some institutions with significant portrait collections have issued catalogs, and other books describe portraits in a region or by special categories. For examples, see the following:

[990] *Catalogue of American Portraits in the New-York Historical Society,* 2 vols. (New Haven: Yale University Press, for the New-York

Historical Society, 1974), which includes information on 2,420 portraits, of which 939 are illustrated.

[991] *Index of Pacific Northwest Portraits,* by Marion B. Appleton (Seattle: University of Washington Press, for Pacific Northwest Library Association, 1972).

[992] *Portraits in the Massachusetts Historical Society: An Illustrated Catalog with Descriptive Matter,* by Andrew Oliver, Ann Millspaugh Huff, and Edward W. Hanson (Boston: Massachusetts Historical Society, 1988).

[993] *Windows on the Past: Portraits at the Essex Institute,* by Andrew Oliver and Bryant F. Tolles, Jr. (Salem, Mass.: Essex Institute, 1981).

A special kind of portraiture were the silhouettes cut by Auguste Edouart. A selection of them is reproduced in [994] *Auguste Edouart's Silhouettes of Eminent Americans, 1839–1844,* by Andrew Oliver (Charlottesville: Published for the National Portrait Gallery, Smithsonian Institution, by the University Press of Virginia, 1977).

There exist a number of works that are guides to pictures of various sorts held by particular depositories.

[995] *Card Catalog of the Boston Athenaeum Print and Photograph Collection* (Boston, G. K. Hall and Company, 1989), which reproduces on microfiche more than 100,000 catalog cards dealing with some 12,000 works produced in the nineteenth century.

[996] *A Catalogue of Portraits and Other Works of Art in the Possession of the American Philosophical Society* (Philadelphia: American Philosophical Society, 1961).

[997] *Finders' Guide to Prints and Drawings in the Smithsonian Institution,* by Lynda Corey Claasen (Washington: Smithsonian Institution Press, 1981). General discussion of materials in various divisions of the Smithsonian.

[998] *Guide to Photographic Collections at the Smithsonian Institution,* vol. 1, *National Museum of American History,* by Diane Vogt O'Connor (Washington: Smithsonian Institution Press, 1989), the first volume in a projected five-part set documenting the Smithsonian's vast holdings of photographs.

[999] *Guide to the Special Collections of Prints and Photographs in the Library of Congress,* by Paul Vanderbilt (Washington: Library of Congress, 1955). Lists 802 collections by name of originator or sub-

ject designation, with an index of proper names and broad subject categories.

[1000] *An Index to the Picture Collection of the American Jewish Archives,* by Jacob R. Marcus (Cincinnati: American Jewish Archives, 1977).

See also *Guide to the Holdings of the Still Picture Branch of the National Archives* [683], which deals with one of the largest depositories of pictures useful for American historians.

A large and widely used collection of pictures for all periods and countries is the Bettmann Archive in New York City, begun by Otto L. Bettmann in the 1930s and since grown to millions of images. The Bettmann Archive also serves as a depository for news photographs taken by United Press International and other news services—a rich source for more recent American history. The Bettmann Archive itself should be contacted about specific holdings.

Index

The index refers in most cases to item numbers, and these numerals are enclosed in square brackets. Some references are to pages; in these cases the letters "p." or "pp." precede the unbracketed numerals. In titles of works, initial articles (*A, An,* and *The*) are omitted, and sometimes the title is given in shortened form.